Faithfully,

Peter M. Wilson

SOUTHERN EXPOSURE
PETER MITCHEL WILSON

The University of North Carolina Press
Chapel Hill, N.C.

The Baker and Taylor Co.
New York

Oxford University Press
London

Maruzen-Kabushiki-Kaisha
Tokyo

Contentment   Elizabeth O'Neill Verner

Southern Exposure

By Peter Mitchel Wilson

Chapel Hill

The University of North Carolina Press

1927

Presses of
EDWARDS & BROUGHTON COMPANY
Raleigh
Printed in the United States of America

TO MY WIFE

Gray Day, Golden Day,—
Alway
Dimidium meæ animæ

FOREWORD

Southern Exposure is a likeable tale told by a lovable man about his own life and the ways of his neighbors and the resurgence of his beloved state.

The gentlest of Carolina gentlemen, a modest, scholarly son, of invulnerable honor and unsullied kindliness, has, with filial piety, written of the brave old Commonwealth that mothered him, lovingly, knowingly—and fairly.

He was born into affluence, plunged into poverty, acquainted with suffering; lived unstained, and happily remains with us, as fine a flower of Southern gentility and chivalry as ever blossomed.

An artist of images and artisan of words, his little book reflects the beauty and purity of his life, and the dignity and manliness of his fellows.

It is a joy to welcome the book and a happiness to read these intimate reminiscences of gentle Peter Wilson.

W. W. FULLER.

HAYMOUNT, N. Y.
October, 1926

AUTHOR'S ACKNOWLEDGMENT

Some of the material appearing in this volume has already appeared, in slightly different form in the Chapel Hill Weekly, the Raleigh News and Observer, and Banta's Greek Exchange. For permission to reprint I am indebted to the editors of these publications.

THE AUTHOR.

CONTENTS

SOUTHERN EXPOSURE

Chapter I

ANTEBELLUM LIFE IN WARRENTON

LIFE gives its prizes to those who play the game skill-fully, with an eye to the goal; and the gate receipts go to those who play the game ruthlessly, with a cynical eye on the rules. The onlooker gets neither the medal nor the purse. But he gets compensation in kind; he enjoys the game. And he has the satisfaction of seeing life as the player, intent on winning, cannot see it.

I have been an onlooker at life—an eager, interested onlooker. Not for a moment of my seventy-odd years have I been bored with it. It is a good game. I have been close enough to some of the spectacular players to watch them make history. But I have never desired to make it myself; I have been content to go back onto the bleachers and join in with the huzzahs or the jeers that greeted the great play. Touching hands with my fellow onlookers has ever been sweeter to me than the solitude of ambition.

In almost four generations of looking-on, I have seen the rules shift many times. The prizes have changed too, and the technique of the play. But the spirit of the contest is ever the same. Life never alters in the fundamentals. And only the stupid player complains that he cannot memorize the new rules.

However the game itself might change, in whatever field it might be scheduled, I have watched always from the same angle. My seat has always been in the bleachers that faced south.

For the last thirty years I have lived in Washington and my daily work has been done at the Capitol where national history was hourly being made. But I have watched even this great national game with my eyes turned steadily to the south; and the players to whom I have come closest have been southern players.

What follows, then, is an impressionistic record of life as viewed by a confessed onlooker over a period of seventy years and more, from comfortable, reasonably sheltered bleachers, with a southern exposure.

The South in general, I think, and North Carolina in particular, I am sure, is intensely personal. You cannot read its history in the black and white print of events; you must interpret it from the vividly colored portraiture of personalities. You can only know North Carolina when you know North Carolinians. Despite the efforts of present day boosters, the state has not yet become a column of proud statistics. And in the days that I have known and loved, it was a commonwealth of undisciplined individualism.

I would like to talk a little about North Carolina before the Civil War. And to do that, I must talk of the people whom I remember in those antebellum days. Warrenton, the town in which my boyhood was spent, was the nucleus of spreading plantations owned by old-time Carolinians of the prosperous, so-called "aristocratic" class. Now, class distinctions in the state have never had the rigidity which they have possessed in Virginia or in South Carolina, possibly because our upper class was smaller and less powerful. The most powerful class in the state, the one which has admittedly struck the note on which the voice of our state has ever been pitched, is the middle class. Upper middle class, perhaps—prosperous and generous. But lacking the intellectual tolerance, the pride of race, the assurance, which mark an aristocracy. North

Carolina's oldest families have mingled freely with this upper middle class, have intermarried with it; and as the state has been indifferent to traditions and careless with heirlooms, it is difficult to put one's finger on any group of families and say, "Here is the best we have."

But I think one can say without misgiving that Warrenton was fairly typical of the best antebellum life of the state. It was typical in this respect anyway—it was uninterested in achievement. It did not ask of a man "What has he done?" It asked, "What sort of a human being is he?" The town, like the state, was intensely personal. Here, then, is a picture of Warrenton and Warrenton folk as I recall them before the final curtain of civil war blotted out the scene.

My very first recollection is dated 1851. It was evening and the carpenters were quitting work on the house which my father built on the northwest corner of the Court House Square. That house, unchanged in appearance, still stands and is owned by friends of our family. One of the carpenters picked up some small blocks from the ends of planks and put them into the lap of my frock, which he showed me how to hold in order to keep the blocks from falling out. My father was standing by and I can remember my delight in the prospect of building a house like his house. We lived in that house on the Court House Square for five years. There my mother taught me my letters and taught me to read. I can remember the life there quite distinctly. And especially is my memory warmed by recollections of the kindly care with which the colored servants surrounded my life and that of my brothers and sister. One quaint illustration of this kindliness recurs in the picture of "Mammy Rena" (Serena) putting sweet potatoes in the ashes and coals at night,

when she tucked us into bed. Then, when we got up in
the mornings, after a new fire had been built, she would
rake the potatoes out of the ashes and break them, divid-
ing them amongst us. They would be steaming hot and
would warm us up, before breakfast on cold winter
mornings.

The slaves who worked on my father's farm at Glenburnie were friendly comrades of my childhood, too. My
father used to take me with him quite frequently when he
would ride out to the farm on business. Once I remember
one of the colored people gave me a little rabbit which he
had caught for me. We did not know how to keep the
rabbit from running away until I could get him home and
we had no string to tie about his neck, but the man who
had caught him stripped a piece of bark from a mulberry
tree and made a string of that. Another time, one of the
farm laborers gave me some partridge eggs which I
treasured proudly. And I can clearly recall my intense
interest in the great baptismal ceremony at the farm
when Mr. McRae, rector of the Episcopal Church in
Warrenton, went out and baptized all of the colored
people who desired it.

Since antebellum life in the South rested on the institution of slavery, it seems fitting to give first place to
memories of the relations existing between those who
were served and those who served, if one is to reconstruct
the life of the period.

The slaves whom I knew seemed entirely happy and
contented. My own father never bought a slave and he
never sold but one. That one was a woman named Maria,
whose husband lived on a neighboring farm from which the
Negroes were removed to Alabama in search of the wealth
of the cotton fields. Maria wanted to go with her husband

and my father arranged for her to do so, as he knew she would be happier. The Civil War ended in April and in May, Maria was back in our "yard," and walked into her old room just as though she had been away on a visit!

My personal feeling for the colored people who lived on our place was one of deep and sincere affection. I used to love to play with the Negro children and to eat with the darkies in their cabins. My great delight was to eat Sunday morning breakfast with Mammy Rena. Her husband, Minor, was an expert plowmaker and he was hired to a big establishment in that line. Saturday evenings he always came home and spent Sunday, returning to work Monday morning. I was perfectly happy when my mother let me eat Sunday breakfast with Mammy Rena and Minor, instead of in our own dining room.

The prevailing attitude in Warrenton toward the colored people was very kindly. There were, of course, instances of unfair treatment but they were not common. The sort of thing written of in *Uncle Tom's Cabin* was usually the result of absentee landlordism—just as the cruelties in Ireland were practiced without the knowledge of the absent English landlords.

One of North Carolina's wealthiest men, who was reputed to own a thousand Negroes, used to tell a story on himself. He was at one of his plantations which he had not visited before. He asked the Negro driving the carriage in which he rode:

"Who owns you?"

"They tells me Mr. ————— owns me," the darky replied; "he owns all of us here."

"What sort of man is he?" came the next question.

"I don' rightly know. I aint never seen him."

"Well, are you treated all right by the overseer?"
pressed the landowner.

"Not so bad and not so good."

Then the darky grew more confidential:

"Looks like Mr. ————— don' care much about his
niggers," he said; "'cause if he did, he'd come see about
'em."

There was a whipping post in Warrenton but the only
man I ever saw whipped was a white man. The good feeling that prevailed in the county between the races is
proved by the fact that among twenty thousand people,
with all the upheaval which the emancipation brought,
there was not a murder committed in the county for
several years after the war and that the one Negro tried
for murder during the post-war period was acquitted.
(In the murder of Dr. Jefferson, a popular physician of
the county, a Negro was suspected, but he was given an
absolutely fair trial and was acquitted.)

Religious life in Warrenton followed the Cavalier rather
than the Puritan traditions. The Anglican Church num-
bered among its communicants practically all of those
whose opinions governed in religious as in secular thought.
The townspeople were regular in their church attendance,
the women especially so. The community's theological
beliefs were simple, what we would today describe as
"fundamentalism." In matters of Christian faith, the
people neither doubted nor discussed. The Episcopal services, while formal, of course, were not ritualistic. The
congregation always sang a psalm, as well as a hymn, and
the minister retired after the service to robe himself in
his Geneva gown before returning to the pulpit for his
sermon. Mr. McRae—the first rector of the Warrenton
church whom I can remember—was a man of decided

talents and of strong personality. He was the strictest
observer of ritual Warrenton ever had. No levity or mis-
behavior was tolerated by him, as I found to my cost on
one occasion when something struck my young risibilities
and I laughed out loud. Mr. McRae paused in the service and said with severity:

"Please remove the child from church."

I was led away in disgrace to the great mortification of
my mother and to my own complete bewilderment.

Later my brother Ben also left the church precipitately,
but in his case the departure was voluntary. Old Dr.
Hodges was the rector then, the personification of benevolent dignity, an imposing, handsome man, and the author
of a book of repute on "Baptism." A circus had visited
the town and in it were the usual cages of wild beasts, including the always ferocious and interesting lion. On the
next Sunday, in reading the scriptural lesson, Dr. Hodges
said in his grave, benignant way:

"There is a lion in the way."

Whereupon Ben promptly bolted, dashing madly down
the church aisle and making a straight line for home,
which he thought was safer than the Sanctuary.

The evangelic churches used to have revivals, but they
were not the big, elaborately staged affairs of the present
day. For one thing, they could not be continued very
late into the evening. At nine o'clock curfew rang for all
the colored people—

"Run, nigger, run;
The pateroller will catch you."

Also, it was not considered wise to have too many of the
emotional black race gathered in a crowd, and this con-

sideration further depleted the numbers on which a re-
vivalist could count.

The simplicity and the final sanity of religious thought
in the community found expression in a small happening
that crosses my memory.

Mr. Goodloe, born and bred in Warrenton, was walking
with a friend one Sunday afternoon when they met a
woman going to the cemetery with her arms full of flowers
to put on the grave of her little child who had lately died.
Both men spoke sympathetically of her distress, but Mr.
Goodloe's companion remarked that he could not understand what she had done that had caused God to punish
her by taking away her innocent child. Mr. Goodloe said:
"Do you think God took her child from her as a punishment?"

"Yes. What other reason could He have had?" was the
reply.

"Then, sir," said Mr. Goodloe, "your God is my devil."

Little can be said of the intellectual life of Warrenton,
and that little is negative. Thinking was social and con-
crete. Warrenton people were more addicted to life than
to literature. And they knew how to live!

Before-the-war life in the South was not luxurious, but
comfortable. The "great mansions" of southern romance
were really just comfortable homes. But the South had
plenty of good, willing service, cheerful service, and this
made for a leisurely life.

Warrenton was justly famous for its housewives, who
took pleasure and pride in the best cooking and in the beautiful service of that cooking. The Warrenton people entertained a great deal, not so much in large parties as in

many and continuous small ones. What we today call "house parties" were popular. Card playing was reserved for the family circle or the gaming table; "card parties" were unknown. At the formal entertainments there was conversation, always supper, nearly always music and dancing. I remember that the town boasted a "Thespian Theatrical Club" which gave amateur plays. J. L. B. had a dancing class; we children derisively called him "Janet Laura." The boys all resented attendance at the dancing school and those who were forced to do the "fancy dances" were especially hostile and obstreperous. We learned the square dances, polka, and schottische. It was at this class that my brother Tom refused to dance with a girl who wore her pantalets unnecessarily long and starched the wrong way. So much for the famed southern chivalry!

There were in the community a number of professional visitors, aristocratic tramps. They were people who belonged to the oldest families in the county, but as a rule they were a little "lacking." Their delight was in going from house to house—and in the days of large plantations that meant considerable distances—and in bringing in the latest small talk from the town or from the last home visited. On one occasion, one of these visitors for a week-without-end was sitting on the porch, enjoying the company of the family then entertaining him, when he saw walking up from the front gate another of the craft who, he knew instantly, was coming with no idea of going. He flew into a rage, stamped his cane upon the floor, took his hat and departed incontinently, saying:

"Here comes that damned gadabout. I'll have none of his company."

These visitors had a county-wide reputation. But in the town of Warrenton itself there was more than one lady of mature age, maid or widow, who had a habit of paying visits late in the evening, but just in time for an invitation to tea or "supper," as it was then called. The hour when the children were due to be tucked into bed was the hour usually chosen by these ladies for their return home and the gentleman of the house or one of the boys was made an escort for this journey in which there was no possible danger. The celerity with which the boys could disappear as soon as supper was over on such occasions was always a puzzle to older members of a family. Once, in our own home, when search was made for an escort for one of these good but itinerant ladies, my mother passed into the garden, under the grape arbor, calling her boys by name in the hope of getting at least one for the errand. Suddenly there was a crash and one of the sticks which made the arbor broke under the weight of Ben, the fat boy of the family, who came tumbling down in a heap, covered with grape vines and defeat. He was immediately drafted for duty. The lady for whom he acted as unwilling escort was a very strict school teacher and not in very high favor with the younger sets. She was crisp in her talk and severe in her manner. She took small note of time, even in its flight, and once when she dropped into our house for tea, she found the association of the household so entirely to her liking that she sent for her trunk and remained a month!

The life of children in those days was very simple but very happy. Toys were not had in the surfeiting abundance that we know today. In my childhood, I remember a few simple toys and a good supply of firecrackers. When my mother and father went to Richmond to the unveiling of Washington's statue, they brought me a new toy, a little game made on the principle of a cribbage board in which one moved toy horses up so many pegs at a time, according to the throw of the dice. Two people played the game, racing the horses against one another. I was very proud of it and took it to school next day to show it to the other boys. First I showed it to Charles Price. His eyes gleamed. He immediately saw possibilities. It was in the chinquapin season, when all the boys came to school with pockets full of chinquapins.

"With this thing we can get all the chinquapins in school!" Charles Price exclaimed.

Then he explained it to me. We would let the boys race the horses and bet on the winner, but before they could do so, they must first pay us a fee. As he set forth the possibilities, I could see them too. That evening Charles and I divided our profits and I went home in great glee to tell my father of our scheme. My father listened very quietly, then he asked gently:

"And what, my son, was Charles's contribution to the undertaking? You say he gets half the profits?"

Gradually my father's meaning dawned on me. I had had my first contact with a promoter. But, of course, what Charles Price contributed was the brains. In later life he continued to contribute them to many plans and became a distinguished lawyer and United States District Attorney.

The antebellum womanhood of the South—woman's position in the community, her share in the responsibili-

ties of the life of the time—this subject requires the turn-
ing of a page, the writing of a fresh chapter. The matter
cannot be touched upon in a paragraph because the whole
discussion has been so obscured by the falseness of romanticism that one must be at some pains to achieve the
clarity of truth. With such purpose, I shall try to make
as photographic a picture as possible of a woman who, by
virtue of her personal qualities, was an outstanding figure
in the life of Warrenton, but who was, God be thanked,
not untypical. That woman was my own grandmother,
Elizabeth Holman Person.

Chapter II

POTRAIT OF A LADY OF THE OLD SOUTH

ELIZABETH HOLMAN PERSON, the daughter of William Person and Elizabeth Holman, his wife, was born on the 5th day of April, 1797, in her father's home, a quaint old house surrounded by fine oak trees and hence unimaginatively called "The Oaks," situated about two miles from the town of Warrenton.

When she was eleven years old, Elizabeth was sent to school, her education up to that time having been guided by her father who was himself an omnivorous reader. At the old Plunkett School in Warrenton she was instructed in English, reading, punctuation, parsing, and handwriting. (Her report cards in these subjects were carefully cherished and are now in the possession of one of her granddaughters.) Later she was advanced to French, Latin, and music; and of course all kinds of fine sewing and fancy work were included in the curriculum.

In 1813 her mother died and Elizabeth went to live with her near-kinswoman, the wife of Governor James Turner. With her young Turner cousins, she completed her education under the guidance of a governess employed in the household.

She was a conscientious student and, young as she was, appreciated her educational opportunities at their true value. Her eagerness to learn and her determination to perform all her schoolgirl tasks creditably laid the sound foundations of her character and made her in later years both a useful person and an interesting social being.

The early death of her mother naturally accentuated her father's influence upon her life and character, an influence which would under any circumstances have been strong because her father's personality was dominant. He lived to be ninety-two years old and so this influence persisted through a large part of her life.

I remember him as a tall, gaunt man, having a face not unlike the prints of John D. Rockefeller. His mouth was disfigured, when I knew him, by a very large scar made by the excision of a supposed cancer by the celebrated surgeon, Dr. McClellan, of Philadelphia. He submitted to this operation (when over seventy years of age) without taking any opiate and when offered a goblet full of brandy, he said:

"No. I have lived a sober man and I will die one."

When asked upon occasion what were the peculiar Person traits, he responded instantly:

"Irascibility of temper and general deviltry."

This coincided with the tradition which no doubt has much truth at the bottom of it that when his daughter Elizabeth was sought in marriage by a certain Mr. Pendleton of Virginia, a young man who had all that romance could exact of a suitor except wealth, he firmly rejected the suit, saying:

"No. My daughter is for no damned poor Virginian. I have quite other plans."

But his practical views of romance did not destroy the strong friendship between himself and his daughter; she was so thoroughly his daughter that she doubtless saw things through his glasses. At any rate, she later married Peter Mitchel, a prosperous Scotchman who had made a business success in America, and whom her father strongly favored as a suitor. Upon her marriage her father settled upon her a large farm near Warrenton and on that farm her husband built for her an attractive home which he called "Elgin" in memory of his Scotch associations.

In enumerating the Person traits, William Person forgot to mention two of the most characteristic. One of these was a lust for land. He himself, so it was said, could ride horseback from the Roanoke River to the Mississippi and sleep on his own lands every night. But, having acquired land, the Persons invariably disposed of it by the English method. They discriminated without variation against the daughters and in favor of the sons in the family who bore the name. So the farm at Elgin, a marriage gift to his daughter, was not given outright, but was entailed upon her son, should she have a son, who was to inherit it upon reaching his majority. Likewise, the other gifts which he made to her were usually merely life interests; the titles to his properties went to her brothers, although she was the child closest to his affections.

Her private reactions to this un-American discrimination between children cannot be recorded because she possessed the second Person trait which her father had failed to mention, namely, a gift for silence. But it was thoroughly characteristic of her that she did not allow resentment to weaken her purpose or distort her affections. Her response to life was ever positive. Such negative emotions as dissatisfaction, envy, resentment, would have cluttered her life and she liked spaciousness and good order.

The atmosphere of the life which she created on the Elgin plantation was pleasantly busy, wholesomely gay. There was the usual liberal hospitality of the period and a number of parties to which the townspeople drove out in the evenings, so that her children all had happy memories of their youthful years. But, under this happy surface, there was the never ending routine of community existence which she capably directed. The early death of her husband and his four years of illness preceding death, threw upon her the responsibility of managing their property. It will be illuminating to those who view the old-time southern woman through the pink and blue veil of romanticism to know something of the responsibilities which fell to the lot of Elizabeth Mitchel and which she met so admirably.

The farm of Elgin consisted of about three thousand acres of land, with the usual orchards, gardens, etc. Within the large yard, away from the lawn and hedges and grove, were the wash house, the weaving rooms, the smoke houses, and all the appurtenances of the domestic needs. For the farm there was a blacksmith shop and blacksmith, a carpenter, a shoemaker, a wheelwright, in short, all the equipment necessary for repairs of farming utensils. About one hundred slaves lived in good, substantial outhouses and were treated with real consideration. They had great respect and love for their mistress, whom they watched managing this property in detail and increasing its value from day to day. She managed a community in which there was all the manufacturing claimed by a New England town. In other words, she produced and converted into usable forms everything which could be grown or made on the property. And to show the quality of the work done on that farm, some of the blankets woven at Elgin are still in existence!

In later years when I described these activities to Dr. North, Director of the Census in the Roosevelt administration, he remarked that the New England town and the southern plantation were corresponding economic units. Thus a woman who directed a fairly large plantation acted in the capacity of what we would today call a town manager.

Elizabeth Mitchel was a feminist, without the self-consciousness of feminism.

But more remarkable than her practical ability was the pragmatic expressions which she gave to her sane, unemotional understanding of human relations—a sanity which we like to believe is a modern development. When her son, Peter Mitchel, reached his majority and came into possession of the Elgin property which she had developed and of which she had had absolute control, she ceased instantly to be the mistress of Elgin and unless called upon for advice she never offered it but left the property to be managed entirely by the then owner! She even moved from Elgin, though her son would have loved to have her stay, and took over the town house belonging to my father who had then moved to his own farm.

This move accomplished two things. It gave her son complete control of his estate; and it gave her a home free from any but domestic responsibilities, where she could come and go as she pleased and could enjoy a measure of leisure after carrying many and complex cares for almost forty years. It was while she was living in this town house that I really came to know her. My sister and I would come in from our father's farm each Monday and stay with our grandmother until Friday evening when school was over for the week. We found her companionable in every way. I remember that some time before I could smoke without question in the presence of my father and mother, my grandmother connived at this indulgence, and sitting upstairs in her room, surrounded by a pleasant,

2

grown-up mist of tobacco smoke, I had many a confidential talk with her, while the disparity between our ages dwindled. She gave me the opportunity—sadly neglected— of knowing many things about many people. She was not in the least censorious but she could tell with a certain quaintness of the failings of people of pretentions.

She was fond of reading newspapers and had decided opinions about public affairs and public men. She was a sound Whig in her political beliefs and had unbounded faith in the wisdom of their leader in North Carolina at that time, the Hon. George E. Badger. Mr. Badger had married Rebecca Turner, one of the cousins in whose home she had lived as a girl, and though his wife had died and he had married again, the association between him and my grandmother remained close and cordial. Every day of her life she read from a big, old-fashioned prayer book given to her by "her friend G. E. B." and in later years I recall going with her (when we were in the state capital, Raleigh, on a visit) to see Mr. Badger who had suffered a paralytic stroke and had retired from public life. I remember how glad he was to see "Betsy Person" and how overcome he was by the memories and associations which the sight of her recalled.

Perhaps it was her confidence in Mr. Badger's leadership and a reflection of his attitude—for he was a particularly sane statesman—that kept her from violence of political opinion. I cannot recall hearing her express any violent opinion, even during the war. Like all the Whigs, she opposed secession but her sympathies were entirely with the South after the breaking out of hostilities, and her two sons and her only nephew were in the Confederate Service from the beginning. But, while never violent, she was strong in the Whig faith, as I can testify from early experience.

In 1857 President Buchanan came to North Carolina to visit the University and make an address at commencement. En route, he stopped for dinner with his old friend and former colleague in the House of Representatives, Weldon N. Edwards, who lived about eight miles from Warrenton. The President's train stopped at the nearest station—Ridgeway, I think—and the President drove from there out to Mr. Edwards's house, where he dined with a company of friends before resuming his journey. Everybody from the county was there to see him arrive. The train came in with the engine all bedecked with ribbons, and I remember that an old Negro man who was "hired out" by his owner to do work about the station and was known as "Depot Sam," was permitted to make a little address of welcome to Mr. Buchanan. The county was intensely Democratic—there were only seventy-six Whigs all told—so the interest in seeing a Democratic President was especially warm. But my grandmother was such an ardent Whig that she had told me she would give me a gold dollar if I would not shake hands with Buchanan. I promised that I would not and I kept the promise and collected my bribe. But when I got to the station and saw all the other children going up to shake hands with him, I bitterly regretted my promise, for even then I had the kind of mind which wanted to do what my fellows were doing.

(An amusing little side light on this adventure occurs to me. Driving over to the station, my father asked me what I thought the President would look like. I said that I thought he would be a tall, thin man, wearing a cutaway coat and a frilled collar, his hair in a queue. That was the picture I had seen in my geography book called "The President's Reception." My father told me that he thought Mr. Buchanan would be a large, bulky man, with gray hair brushed back, minus a queue; that he would probably wear an ordinary summer suit—no formal cutaway; and that he would carry his head a little to one side. When I saw the President, I thought my father was very wonderful to have imagined him so perfectly. Buchanan had a stiff neck and always held his head a bit to one side, a fact which my father had of course known.)

This slight anecdote will illustrate the warmth of my grandmother's political loyalty, a loyalty which sought to transmit itself to her infant grandchildren!

Her interest in public affairs was ever vivid. She was not one of those who could ignore the fall of an empire, if the dinner roast were burning. Even now, I can remember the graphic description which she gave me of the receipt of the news of the Battle of New Orleans. While a ball was being danced out at the principal tavern of the town, an express messenger dashed up and shouted the tidings that Jackson had defeated the British. Instantly all was a glorious turmoil. She said: "I was playing billiards"—an unusual accomplishment for women in that day—"when I heard the news and rushed out onto the gallery to join in the rejoicing." As she described the town, touched with the thrill of victory, the scene lived again for me, recreated by her own thrilling sense of the significance of that victory.

She read a good many books and delighted in going over to "the old place" and browsing in her father's library. She sometimes took me with her and I recall that it was among her father's books that I first saw a copy of

Uncle Tom's Cabin; and that when I began to read it, my grandmother suggested to me that I put it aside until I was a little older. My mother has told me, with no little amusement, of her girlhood recollections of the excitement in their household when one of Sir Walter Scott's new books would arrive. My grandfather had ordered in advance every book which Sir Walter should write, and as soon as one would come, my grandmother would read it aloud to the whole family.

But she liked what might be called "lighter" reading too! Her grandchildren used to tease her a good bit about her love for the Memphis paper and her excuse for some absence on the ground that she had found a "perfectly beautiful murder story" in the Memphis *Appeal,* which had made her lose track of time. (In those days homicide was a matinée performance in Memphis, which had not lost its character as a Mississippi steamboat town.)

Of a reserved disposition, my grandmother had comparatively few close friends but she was most faithful to them and paid small heed to any criticism or gossip about them. Once when there was a great dissension in the church to which she was very much attached, she took the part of the rector and would not allow any one to say anything to his discredit in her hearing.

She was always interested in helping people who showed a disposition to help themselves. As an instance, she employed a young man named Jack Rivers, who had a most meagre education and who was quite solitary, to superintend the "old place," as the former home of her father was known in the family; and she arranged for him to take time enough from his duties to attend Mr. Dugger's school and get as much education as he could take. Of course, he was awkwardly placed, a grown man amongst boys in their teens, but he had the courage to undertake it and my grandmother had perceived that he had the courage. He carried out his contract in good faith and on her side my grandmother paid his tuition, gave him a home at the "old place" and paid him a living wage. I myself was his schoolmate when he had his position in the beginners' class, and looking back, I can see that the courage he showed in this anomalous situation was of the same quality as the spirit which later led him to his last resting place on a Virginia battlefield.

It would be easy to illustrate how much good she did and with what little ostentation, and how kind she was to all without any display. She had the sort of generosity which is subtler than mere open-handedness. Her spirit was generous.

But lest she seem to have none of the lovable weaknesses of human nature, let me record her singular concession to the vanities. Because her hair turned white quite early, she kept it clipped close to her head, where it grew in soft, white ringlets, and wore over it a dark wig. Persons who like to divide traits of character and qualities of mind on a sex basis will now acquit her of any taint of masculinity!

This is a portrait of a lady of the old South, painted in true colors and with no retouching. I have chosen a portrait from my own family gallery because only thus could I vouch for its authenticity. And my purpose in presenting it at all is to call attention to the strange contrast which it offers to the more conventional pictures of pretty, vapid female creatures which the romanticists have hung in the galleries of southern tradition.

Chapter III

NORTH CAROLINA SCHOOLS OF THE FIFTIES

Education in the middle years of the nineteenth century had none of the elaborate equipment thought necessary by pedagogues of the twentieth century. The schools of my recollection would seem crude and poor to the modern educator. The curricula were simple and the methods of instruction were elemental. In place of the psychological tests and treatments which are today given to the recalcitrant student, we had the switch and the dunce cap. The old education was doubtless unscientific, but I am not so sure that it was inferior as a basis for social morality and an introduction to human relationships. The swift and inevitable punishment which overtook an unruly boy at least taught him a wholesome respect for rules. There was a clarity in the boy's perception of cause and effect, and there was a toughening of moral fibre. Both of these things were needed later in the devastating days of Reconstruction, when those same boys had become men. I doubt if the enervating ease of modern education could have prepared them to fight their way through the hardships which tested their manhood.

My mother taught me to read and to make my letters. But my first experience at school came in 1856. We had moved from the town of Warrenton, then, and were living at my father's farm, Glenburnie, a few miles from town. It was more than a mile, across a creek and through fields and woods, to what we called the "country school" or "field school," kept by an Irishman named Kelly, who taught us reading, writing, and arithmetic. He was very particular about the cleanliness of our slates and every day we had to take the slates down to a spring and wash them thoroughly, drying them in the sun. Woe to the boy who tried the lazy method of spitting on his slate!

The school itself was a log building, daubed with mud; windows of spaces made by omitted logs, battened down by a plank fitting more or less—never more. There was a fireplace with capacious mouth, soapstone back, and runners like andirons. Plank seats ran around three sides of the room and on the fourth was an inclined shelf which served as a common writing desk.

One of the colored boys on our place, Albinus ("'Binus," I always called him), who was about ten years old was assigned to the duty of accompanying me to school in the mornings. I remember one day when I had set off reluctantly and under protest, it came to me in crossing the creek that it would be a good plan to slip in and get wet so that I would have to go home. So I quietly fell off the log which formed a primitive bridge, and got a thorough soaking up to my arm pits. 'Binus was wiser than I and would not commit himself to this voluntary immersion, but he was willing enough to turn homeward with me, carrying the bucket which contained my dinner. When we got home and I narrated my "accident," my mother said it was too bad, instructed Mammy Rena about putting clean, dry clothes on me, and then told 'Binus that we must take up our journey again and make our excuses at the school as best we could. Arrived at school, I was given extra lessons by way of punishment for my tardiness. In those days persons charged with the responsibility of rearing a child were less fearful of colds in the head, but more fearful of obstinacy in the will!

Natually my memories of those first school days are a bit misty. And the clearest and most pleasurable one is not of an educational nature. It relates to the wonderful hot rolls, the honey and milk, which our nearest neighbor, Mrs. Bobbitt, always offered me when I came through her front yard on my way home in the afternoons. Her boys were bigger than I and they used to bring me home, 'Binus having returned to the farm after seeing me safely to school in the morning.

After a while the frequent occasions upon which Mr. Kelly would send word that school would not keep that day attracted my youthful curiosity and I tried in vain to find out from my father what was the occasion of his being too unwell to carry on his school duties. Finally it leaked out amongst the boys that a taste for "the critter" would overcome him periodically and that he would not be in condition to appear before his school. So at the end of that year the neighbors who clubbed together to pay the expenses of the school—including, of course, Mr. Kelly's salary—decided that education at that point would be temporarily suspended. And the following year I was entered at Mr. Dugger's school, an academy for boys in Warrenton.

John E. Dugger, the head of the Academy, was a young man at that time, hardly any older than some of the "old boys" in the school. But he was a college bred man who had taken second honors at Chapel Hill, and was entirely capable of teaching his pupils anything that they proposed to learn. He made the academy an important school and while it was never in a class with Bingham's or with Dr. Wilson's at Alamance, yet it was on a much higher plane than any school in its section of the state. So thoroughly did Mr. Dugger put his mark upon the institution that it became known as Mr. Dugger's School, instead of its old and ridiculously awkward name— "Warrenton Male Academy."

We were all a little afraid of him for he was a strict disciplinarian, though he had not at that time developed the choleric disposition which long pedagogic habit produced in him later. Some of the big boys gave him considerable trouble with their fighting proclivities and I remember a talk that he gave to the assembled school on the subject of fighting. He told us that his own father had been killed in a duel by George Coke Dromgoole, Member of Congress from a Virginia district; that he could recall how terrible his father's death had been—a death by violence; and that it was the result of the bad habit of dueling which was but the outgrowth of another habit—quickness to give and take insult. He carefully disclaimed any intention of teaching us to *take* an insult, but he urged upon us the necessity for learning not to *give* an insult.

The community took great pride in the success of the school and great personal pride in Mr. Dugger's proficiency. It was a serious break in Warrenton's educational story when he felt it his duty to enter the Confederate Army. He resigned his position, gathered around him quite a number of men, and formed a company which was incorporated into the Eighth North Carolina troops. After going through the usual preliminary training, they were early brought into real warfare when, after a battle of importance in its consequences but of no great proportions, the Confederate forces including Mr. Dugger's regiment were captured and Mr. Dugger returned to Warrenton, a paroled soldier. I can recall the interest with which the people followed him around to get him to tell the story of the battle and the capture. He scrupulously observed his parole, wearing only citizen's clothes until exchanged, when he entered the service again and continued as a soldier (of merit and gallantry) until the war came to an end.

In the fall of 1865 Captain Dugger (as he was now known) gathered about him such students as could pay or promise to pay and again put the school upon its feet. He continued this good work for ten years, when he was called to head the first graded school established in the capital of the state. As principal of the school in Raleigh, Captain Dugger did fine pioneer work, but his disposition had become autocratic and he showed an ineptitude for acting in concert with the authorities of the school. He had never been a man under authority and this new condition was irksome to him. So it was that in a few years he resigned and returned to Warrenton, which was his natural habitat and where there was no disposition to tame his personality. He reëstablished his school there, where it again succeeded; and he followed his vocation until he was suddenly called into the night.

While small of stature, Captain Dugger was graceful, well formed and handsome to an unusual degree. He acquired the habit, as a dominie, of hectoring and he carried this in his tone to a considerable extent in his dealings with men. He was unnecessarily free-spoken—even to God—and said most unexpected things at unexpected times. As an instance, there is the tale of a dinner party at his home which was preceded (in the old-time fashion) by a blessing, in the course of which Captain Dugger startled his guests by interpolating between conventional invocations this plea—

"Help us, Oh Lord, to forgive our enemies of all sorts and conditions, even, Oh Lord, such damned rascals as ——— and ———."

The blanks which here appear were filled in with the specific names of two members of the board governing the Centennial School, men whom he supposed to be especially inimical to him and whom he mortally detested. One of the two thus reluctantly recommended for Divine forgiveness was, amusingly enough, a beacon light of his particular denomination.

When Captain Dugger left Raleigh, he left a host of friends who enjoyed his peculiarities and rather gloated over his stiff knee before authority and his laxity in obedience to established customs and prejudices. His enemies—whose enmity was largely imaginary—bade him Godspeed and his friends beckoned him to come again.

But this tale of his pedagogic career is a digression from my own story of North Carolina schools in the fifties and sixties. To return.

January 1, 1862, found the town of Warrenton with an overflowing population. It was a most convenient as well as most hospitable haven for the refugees from the vicinity of Newport News, Hampton, Norfolk, and parts of Eastern Carolina, then in possession of the Federal troops.

The schools were filled with girls and small boys; the youth had volunteered. There were practically no men left to carry on the schools for boys and co-education was the only resort. It was decided that I was to go to boarding school and the institution selected was the Bingham School which had then, as now, great reputation both in the state and throughout the South. It was commonly reported, too, that there was small danger of a boy being spoiled at Bingham's by any sparing of the rod. My father had written to Mr. Bingham and made application to have me received as a pupil in the school and in course of his letter had mentioned the necessity for my being put under strict discipline. Mr. Bingham's answer was short and to the point. He acknowledged receipt of the letter and said in a line—

"I quit breaking wild colts ten years ago."

This concluded the correspondence. Shortly afterwards, however, Mr. Bingham wrote a very courteous letter saying that there was a vacancy in the school and if I could come promptly I might avail myself of the opportunity. I did so and my father and I set out at once for this quaint establishment, twelve miles south of Hillsboro.

I say "quaint" because while it consisted of a comfortable schoolhouse, the boys were cantoned or quartered in farm houses around about in squads of eight.

Mr. Bingham was the second of the name to have a school of distinction. His father, an honor graduate of Glasgow, had carried on such a school from 1788 until he died, and William J. Bingham had inherited and succeeded to all of its excellence and traditions. He had two sons who were his assistants, Col. William Bingham, author of the Bingham series of Latin books and a most accomplished scholar, and Maj. Robert Bingham, who, to the reputation of a gallant soldier serving with distinction through the Civil War, added achievements as an educator which have given to the Bingham School a really national reputation.

William J. Bingham, head of the school when I was there, was a martinet in discipline but strictly just. If he thought it necessary, he would thrash (as he called it) the largest boy in the school as quickly as he would a mere lad. His Irish pugnacity made him prefer a real fight and he never hid behind the excuse that he was administering punishment for the benefit of the punished and greatly to the sorrow of the punisher.

To illustrate his impatience with any sort of lying: He surprised his Monday morning class once by asking offhand if any of the boys had robbed any birds' nests. (He disliked extremely this cruelty to the songsters and had forbidden it under penalties.) He ordered all boys who had robbed birds' nests to hold up their hands. Only two pairs of hands went up. He then proceeded with great deliberation to thrash all those boys who had not put up their hands because his psychology taught him that they had lied and that the two pairs of hands had alone been raised for the truth!

Like Mr. Dugger, he disapproved of fighting and he had an odd cure for it. For some reason not worth mentioning, a friend and I while studying our lessons under the Big Poplar (famous all through that country) concluded to disagree and finally worked ourselves up to what we used to call a fist and skull fight. Unfortunately for us, Mr. Bingham was passing through the grounds and saw the fight. He ordered us at once to "the mahogany" as the dungeon of punishment was called, and pretty soon he appeared there with two stout dogwood switches. He made us take off our jackets and fall to with all our might and main. After we had worn out the switches and had got enough of it, he asked us if we were satisfied and added that if we were he was entirely so, but that he was quite ready to repeat the punishment whenever we repeated the offense.

In 1863 the school was converted into a military school under an act of the North Carolina legislature and the boys in addition to their school work were required to protect the school property and the bridges in the neighborhood by standing guard over them at night, and to drive off the bands of deserters and marauders who were prowling through the Piedmont country heading for the protection of the mountain fastnesses. The military features were carried out with all the strictness peculiar to that class of schools and turned out excellent material for the Confederate service as the cadets became of military age.

The curriculum included Latin, Greek, Mathematics and English. Great stress was laid upon the study of Latin. Mr. Bingham held the belief that of all grammars, Latin grammar was the best, and he did not even teach English grammar. Col. William Bingham wrote the full Latin grammar with exercises and required the lesson for the next day to be written on the blackboard by boys who wrote the best hands and copied by all the students. Few textbooks were printed in the South and the supply was exhausted. There were no books to be had. This method proved not only that Latin could be taught without books but that it could be most effectively taught. At the end of each session, the students had their notes stitched together and these notes constituted Bingham's Latin Grammar. The same methods were applied to Mathematics. There were Greek grammars and to spare, as they were used only by the higher classes.

In the last year of the war Confederate money had become so valueless that the farmers who took the boys to board declined to receive it. They could not well have done otherwise, though Mr. Bingham always accepted Confederate money for tuition and at the smallest possible advance over the original charges. The Binghams

were conscientious Confederates at any cost. In order
to pay for his board, each boy had to bring a substitute
for money in the form of bacon or flour or other table
necessaries.

Through all these difficulties the school never missed a
day. Three of Mr. Bingham's kinsmen, Major W. B.
Lynch and the two Tom Norwoods, Big Tom and Little
Tom, furloughed on account of wounds, took the chairs
of Robert Bingham and William Bingham. But when the
boys disbanded for the Christmas holidays preceding
General Lee's surrender, Mr. Bingham announced that
it was thought best to have the school reassemble at Mebane. This step was taken because there were now so
many Red Strings (sympathizers with the North) in the
Oaks neighborhood that there was constant danger of interruption of work for the boys in a military school.
Colonel Bingham had given his chief labor to the building
of the barracks, as the log houses were called, at Mebane
to which the operations of the school were to be transferred
in the January term. The cadets dispersed in the Christmas holidays. The fall of Fort Fisher, the rumbling of the
collapse of the Confederacy, and the sweep of the Federal
army of General Sherman through southeastern North
Carolina defeated the plans for opening the school exercises in the beginning of the new year. So the cadets were
furloughed and made their way to their several homes as
best they could. I never went back to the Bingham School
at Mebane as a student and only saw it as a visitor, in
later years, watching it grow from stout log houses to comfortable frame cottages. It was always a real school.

I never knew Bingham School boys in after life who did
not carry with them a sincere respect for Mr. Bingham,
both as a thorough teacher and as a just man.

Chapter IV

CHAPEL HILL AFTER THE WAR

THE months following the surrender of the Confederate armies were filled with confusion and distress. To the physical hardships which the final years of the war had brought, was now added the spiritual burden of defeat. But there was still a measure of social and political order. Southern territory was under military control; was subject to the armies which on the battlefield had learned to respect the soldiers whom they finally defeated. Not yet had the South been abandoned to the unbridled passions of noncombatants, to the searing horror of Reconstruction.

There was clear apprehension that an epoch had closed and that a new and strange one was opening. But the survivors of the lost civilization did not sit down like so many Mariuses in the ruins. Practically every man took up immediately the duty of providing for and protecting his family. In spite of the new difficulties in the matter of farm labor, fairly decent crops were planted and harvested. And with the coming of the frost, parents again took up the responsibility of equipping their children with the best education possible. Pitifully small resources were strained to pay tuition fees and to enter the young people in such schools as had survived the debacle.

In October, 1865, I went to Chapel Hill. After a night in Durham, (now a breeding ground for millionaires, but then a small railroad way station), I rode over to Chapel Hill in a hack driven by a charming bandit, if appear-

3

ances counted for anything. In the hack were another young student, and a trustee of the University, class of '38, who was going to confer with Governor Swain, President of the University, on a proposed visit to Andrew Johnson, in regard to North Carolina affairs.

The hack stopped at the home of Governor Swain and we all got out. The title "President of the University" always made way for his older title of "Governor," won by his former service as chief magistrate of the state. But to the students he was known as "Old Bunk," outrageous abbreviation of Buncombe, the name of his home county, and a name which had already acquired its world-wide significance through the Congressional activities of the famous "gentleman from Buncombe."

My first impression of Old Bunk was of a tall, shambling, bandy-legged man, with a strong and kindly face. He told me in a guttural tone and out of the righthand corner of his mouth more about my forebears than I remembered ever having heard, and he wound up with the hope that I would do better than my uncle who, about twenty years before, had been demoted from Chapel Hill to Princeton for reasons satisfactory to all parties. The Governor then sent me to one A. Mickle, the bursar, a gentle old man who, through fair peace and hideous war, had never failed to make his figures speak the truth. From him I made my way to the campus, lair of the sophomores, and took my first lesson in the humanities, if I may so call them.

And so this was Chapel Hill!

Then, as now, it was officially known as The University of North Carolina. But now the title is accurate. Then it was as unreal as were the stately phrases of the diplomas. Chapel Hill was a college; it was a small, compact

body of men who, through "four years of organized leisure," found three things: first, a recipe for seasoning life;
second, congenial friendships; third, the foundations for
the then recognized professions, law, medicine, theology.
But certainly the Chapel Hill of those days was not a
place where one was inspired with enthusiasm for abstract
learning; it was filled with neither the impersonality of
philosophy nor the neutrality of science. It was not a
university.

Languages, especially the dead ones, and mathematics
were stressed in the curriculum. And the grave philoso-
phies of logic and morals were important as corridors to
the legal profession, which in turn was the high road to
politics, and politics was the mecca of education at Chapel
Hill. Students glanced briefly at the sciences but science
was not in vogue.

There was an easy sociability about the place, what
one of Barrie's baffled characters calls "that damn charm."
If it did not breed deep scholarship, if it did not lay up
great stores of learning in thoughtless heads, it leavened
agreeably everyday life and Sundays too.

The Class of '65 was the most heterogeneous class ever
received at the college up to that time. In the first place
there were the men just released from the army, only a
few years older than the other students by the calendar,
but dark ages older in point of experience and suffering.
From the rolls of its student body, Chapel Hill had sent a
battalion into the field. They came back now, a platoon,
to take up a broken life. They were line and staff officers,
subalterns, and privates of high degree; they became, many
of them, leaders of the Invisible Empire—and in that time
the members of the Empire were not the empirical Hes-

sians of politics who wear the mask today, but were helpers of the helpless.

Next, there were the graduates of the recognized preparatory schools, Bingham's, Graves's, Horner's, Wilson's, and the lesser, but sometimes equal, nests. Some of these boys plumed themselves on their superior training and some of them were destined to fall like Dædalus—was not he the first overconfident aviator?

And last, there was a miscellaneous lot of boys who thought much more about getting to Chapel Hill than they thought of what they would do, once there.

The English schools had a system of fagging, which carried with it a sort of menial meaning; the military and classical schools had a kind of purgatory called hazing; but Chapel Hill had a system of deviling, that is to say, roasting well and rubbing in cayenne pepper. A freshman had to go through this ordeal. He was made the butt of countless jokes, teased until he was sore, and subjected to many small indignities, such as being made to enter the chapel through the back doorway in order to get the religious sustenance to which he was entitled. The rules for freshmen were invented, of course, by the sophomores, of whom Dr. James Phillips, dean of the faculty, once remarked, "I do not know of a more disagreeable human being than a six-weeks sophomore." One of these rules forbade any freshman to enter chapel unless he had on a coat; if he were so juvenile as still to wear "jackets," then he was too young for college, the sophomores held. George Winston and I were about the smallest boys in the freshman class and we, neither of us, possessed an adult coat. In the post-war state of our family finances, it was obviously impossible for us to acquire such coats. So we put our heads together and finally evolved a scheme. The faculty required that we attend chapel; the sophomores forbade our attendance in jackets without tails. So we pinned towels to our jackets and with these long white tails hanging behind us, we went to our devotions. George Winston has served as president of three colleges since those far-off days. But to whatever dignities he has attained, he can never have achieved greater solemnity than he wore as he discreetly entered the backdoor of chapel with a towel flapping behind him.

During my pilgrimage through the lower classes I never saw a game of cards played except for amusement. There may have been some gambling, but I never saw it, and as I came from a community where it was not only a pastime, but too often a profession, I think I would have recognized it.

There was some drinking, but no drunkenness. I certainly cannot recall seeing students so far gone as not to be able to plumb the middle of the road—that famous test of sobriety instituted by one of North Carolina's great chief justices. At the night suppers, of course, there was convivial drinking. We read of rare Falernian in our Horace and we sought a similar exaltation of spirit in the more odorous product of our own maize. On occasion we had some old Nick Williams, memory of which stirs one to fresh revolt against the iniquity of sumptuary legislation. And on one very rare occasion we watched a President of these United States (or rather, a President of the very disunited states of that period) quaff a goblet of Kentucky nectar in the second story southwest corner room of the old South Building. (Remember—that was before the nation had dried up into "one vast, awful Kansas.")

President Andrew Johnson was in the state in 1867 to attend the belated unveiling of a monument to his father in the Raleigh cemetery, and he was invited to the commencement exercises of the University. Every honor was paid him and in return he evidenced his own friendliness by recalling in his public speech the kindness which he had met in Chapel Hill forty-one years before, when footsore and hungry, making his difficult way to his future home in Tennessee, he had literally begged his bread!

The President was the guest of Governor Swain, an honest but misguided teetotaler, who visited his vagaries on his guests. It was hot—commencement time is always hot. And the President was in continuous attendance upon the various ceremonies. Finally he escaped from officialdom and wandered about the campus with a group of the college boys. Knowing his fondness for a "nip," one of the boys suggested that there was a bottle of real Kentucky whiskey in the dormitory. All of us—including the President—trooped upstairs in the old South; there was great scurrying for ice, sugar, and the makin's. The President drained a generous glass, then called for another. He was athirst and the friendly hospitality of the boys was uncritical. But I do not mean to intimate that he had too much, for he did not. Just enough to lift his spirit above the heat and the weariness of life on parade . . . . to let it float away from the animosities and nagging responsibilities on a sort of magic carpet.

Dancing was popular at Chapel Hill, then as now. The commencement ball was the final expression of the social life on the Hill and attracted young women from far and wide in the state.

The national game of baseball had invaded the South and was displacing the games previously in favor with the larger boys, cat, bandy, etc. Even the dignified juniors joined in the baseball games and there was soon a "team" which beat Raleigh and the older baseball clubs of the state. I remember the high spirited games, with especially fine catching. The umpire by common consent was Richard H. Lewis, a freshman. He had been lame from his childhood and this was the only way in which he could take part in the games. His decisions were law and there was never an appeal from them. First in class, first in conduct, and first in the confidence of his fellows, he began; and he has never slacked up in his good work. To no one man does North Carolina owe a greater debt for its present security and enlightenment than it owes to Richard Lewis.

But in those days the college heroes were not athletes, at least not in the South. In North Carolina one rose to fame by way of the hustings. Oratory was the supreme gift. And college life, being a sort of rehearsal for the life to come, placed an equal emphasis on skill in debate.

There were two debating clubs at Chapel Hill, the Dialectic Society and the Philanthropic. They divided the students between them on a fairly rigid geographical basis. The boys from the west were Dis, the boys from the east were Phis. Just why these societies should have been secret, it is hard to tell, but they were solemnly so. Of course, their guarded secrets, like the curtained debates of executive sessions in our national Senate, were in the end better known to those without than to those within. By processes of gradual selection, the Dis and the Phis chose declaimers for class exercises at commencement and there was great rivalry between them to furnish more and better speakers. I have known debates to last all night to great weariness of the flesh but with

oratorical spirit undiminished. Can any one wonder that
our southern solons today hold the Thermopylæan Pass
against all fights for cloture of debate in our parliamentary
proceedings?

The debating clubs or literary societies, as they were
known, included all students in their membership; but
there was a further subdivision into voluntary social
cliques called Greek letter clubs or fraternities. There
was a very pronounced feeling against the Greek letter
clubs on general and sensible grounds. The Grecians
called this sour grapes. The "barbarians" called the
powerful little phalanxes self-made aristocrats. Neither
could conclusively prove a case. But at least the clubs
served one good purpose. Like the literary societies, they
were effective lines of quick communication between the
faculty and the student body. And authority needed all
the props it could find just then, for war breeds lawlessness
and Chapel Hill had not escaped the post-war restlessness.
How could it have escaped? Think of what we first-
comers saw when we matriculated in 1865. Actually the
alcoves of the college library were filled with straw bed-
ding and stable litter left by the detachment of Federal
cavalry, recently departed, which had converted the alcoves into stalls for their horses! In our Roman histories
we had read of the horse that was made a consul. But
never before, surely, had a horse been a student. With
sights like these before our eyes, we younger boys could
hardly rise to a fine aloofness from political passions.
And the older boys, the ones who had served in the army,
had yet to adjust themselves to a mild, academic authority which held no bayonet with which to enforce its decrees.

There were many impetuous outbreaks. Once when a
large meeting of Negroes, pitiable, but dangerous in their

ignorance, was held in an upstairs lodge room in the town, the students dispersed it when it became violent. Several students were injured, one almost fatally, and many Negroes were shot and the stairway to the house destroyed. The affair caused great excitement and Governor Swain had to visit the military authorities in Raleigh to persuade them not to send troops to the town. Such outbreaks interrupted the studies scarcely begun and made it difficult for the saner students and the faculty to control the course of daily work.

There was an undue amount of rough play, too. Practical jokes were apt to be carried much too far. As for instance, when a group of young wretches actually put gunpowder under the rostrum of a mild-mannered professor and blew him up. It was not a fatal dose of gunpowder, but it was an exceedingly alarming one. And the incorrigibles who administered it and who thought it amusing to imitate the Orsini bombs which had been hurled at Napoleon would have faced a grand jury but for the kindly professor's interference in their behalf.

The tale of "Old Tige's" generous act of forgiveness is a fitting introduction to a picture of the faculty which struggled not only with our coltish spirits and our obstinately ignorant minds, but fought at the same time a brave and losing fight against grinding poverty and every imaginable discouragement. There were only nine of them holding the fort, but they set the house of their defense very high.

Chapter V

UNIVERSITY FACULTY OF THE SIXTIES

THE Chapel Hill Nine. Sir James Barrie has made the faculty of Edinburgh in the seventies immortal with his essays on "The Edinburgh Eleven." The Chapel Hill Nine can, of course, gain no such fame from my inadequate words. But they do not need it. They immortalized themselves. Perhaps the very existence of the University of North Carolina today, certainly the continuity of the university's traditions, is a monument to those unpretentious, simple, fearless men who, with one exception, kept the faith unto the end. And even if one of them finally found the fight too much for his failing spirit, still one could count nine by including Governor Swain, "Old Bunk," as one of the faculty. Surely no one ever loved Chapel Hill with a greater devotion than his.

These men were not great inspirational teachers. (Later experience at the University of Edinburgh showed me the difference between a professor who teaches by the book and a professor who uses a textbook simply as a spring board from which he dives into the very middle of his subject to bring up fresh treasure.) But they constituted a most competent faculty. They were good drill masters in their particular subjects. And surely they more than compensated for what they failed to teach us of the humanities by what they taught us of humanity at its best and truest. They were serving almost without pay; the university now had no source of income except the meagre tuition fees of the students. Their circum-

stances were so really desperate that special provision
had to be made for permitting them to cut firewood from
the university trees. More than half of them had come
from without the state, several actually were northern
men. But as they had shared the old prosperity, so they
continued to share the dangers of warfare and the suffering of defeat. Forgetting their personal discomforts, they
labored to mold a difficult generation and to keep untarnished the traditions of a great school. There used to
be a whisper among the boys that whenever the bottom
of the bins appeared in the homes of the professors, the
ravens came as in Elijah's time. I will not vouch for the
truth of this, but I believe it. Surely no men ever deserved miraculous intervention more than they!

It was the personality of the teachers rather than the
college courses that counted.

The dean of the faculty was Dr. James Phillips. He
was an Englishman—hence called by the boys "Old
Bull"—and had served in the British military service,
having been one of the guards over Napoleon on the "Bellerophon" when the great Emperor was in transit to St.
Helena. Resigning from the Service, Dr. Phillips had
come to America where he taught school in the North,
until his election to the North Carolina faculty in 1826.

He was a small, bashful man with the idea—to us absurd—that there was still much mathematics for him to
learn. He taught Pure Mathematics and Natural Philosophy. One of the irrespressible juniors, Pat Winston,
once asked him:

"Doctor Phillips, when you stood guard over Napoleon
on the 'Bellerophon,' how did he look?"

"Looked like he didn't like it much," was the laconic
reply and then the doctor's spectacles twinkled.

I never had a class under him and the only service I was ever able to do him was to help Eugene Morehead make him comfortable when he fell dead in chapel, just as he started to pray for Chapel Hill. The service he did us was to show us how a great master of the most exact science could go out into a Space he had not measured.

Dr. Charles Phillips, who taught Mixed Mathematics as it was termed, or Applied Mathematics, was known as "Fatty." He was structurally much after the model of Henry VIII, but with a countenance as different from the cynical monarch's as it could possibly be. He had by far the biggest chair at the University and so completely filled it that a handful of adjunct professors could have been concealed in his pockets, *a la Gulliver*. He taught so fast and thought so fast that only the precious few could follow him. Personally, I could only see the wide expanse of his back, far, far ahead. When my mother came up to Chapel Hill at commencement time, she asked, with gentle maternal solicitude, about my progress.

"Madam," said Fatty, "your son knows less mathematics than any human being I have ever seen."

He was combative and delighted in bowling over interference. There is on record only one instance when he was nonplussed. Calling a student whose performances were never shining, he began this proplem:

"If a ship sails . . . ."

"Stop right there, Dr. Phillips. I never could do one of those ship sailing sums. They upset my stomach," said the boy solemnly. The suggestion was too much for the professor who had no come-back.

Anything in the line of philosophy was a delight to him, and he had rare gifts in applying the philosophy of Christ. He practiced Charity and it came easy to him to preach it. A reverse procedure but, as he proved, more satisfactory than the usual one. I never knew a student who was not a better man for his influence.

A. D. Hepburn held the chair of Metaphysics and Logic. He looked upon his students as syllogisms whose premises he could vary as the conclusions required. If there had been enthusiasm in his classes, he would doubtless have analyzed it as an interesting phenomenon but it would have made him personally uncomfortable. In seeking to teach youth to think coldly, he was, of course, tackling a hopeless task. And in his own self-abnegation, his fidelity to a dying institution, he was himself a refutation of all logic and a justification of the most unreasoning faith.

John Kimberley, familiarly known as "Old Kim" (the appellation "old" was given most professors not because of their senility but because of our affection) was professor of Chemistry. He was looked upon with mingled awe and respect. First, because he was accused of being a scientist, and because the accusation was backed up by testimonials from Harvard and Berlin. Then an insidious rumor had it that he alone of the faculty had an income aside from his class fees. Lastly, it was whispered that he had given a dinner to some seniors and juniors at which wine had flowed. This gave great offense, not for the alleged moral reasons which are assumed these latter days, but because the hedges and byways had not been beaten to fetch in the uninvited of the upper classes. (Of course, no freshmen aspired—hence we were uncritical.)

The surest way for a member of the Latin class to incur the suspicion of Dr. Hubbard ("Old Hub," for short) was to call him "Professor." He had deserved and received a high degree from a high college and he did not like it confused with a title that was indiscriminate. Old Hub was what General Cox used to call a "high man." He always treated his students as fine gentlemen. He could think in Latin or in Greek and could turn them into rhythm too, if one liked. While we may not have attained to any alarming familiarity with those dead tongues, we did learn from Dr. Hubbard to feel the romance of their storied phrases. He taught us still to love Lalage, laughing sweetly, speaking sweetly. He had wit, too, and was not stingy with it when provoked. There was one student in his classes who thought it humorous to feign sleep. When one of the boy's desk mates started to wake him for recitation, the doctor said:

"Oh, don't. Let him sleep. He's vastly more intelligent when he's asleep then when he's awake!"

Hildreth H. Smith, professor of romance languages, was known as "Old Tige." Never was a more glowing misnomer, for while he had proved his courage once by a daring rescue of persons trapped in a fire, yet a milder mannered man never lived. It was Old Tige who was blown up in the gunpowder plot and that episode bears the indelible print of his gentleness, for he was the first to forgive the unforgivable scamps who perpetrated the outrage. He was a scholar rather than a teacher and had a working knowledge of half a dozen languages, which was just five more than any of his students ever had. His impetuousness often bumped him up against his class and the result was sometimes amusing. Once, I remember, he said to a restless student:

"Mr.————, please resume your seat, leave the room or stay where you are."

And he was a thoroughly surprised man when the student, after reflecting upon the redundant alternatives, said, "Well, Professor, I think I'll stay where I am."

Manuel Fetter, condensed as usual into "Old Fet," was a Pennsylvania Dutchman who had somehow escaped being a Lutheran preacher to become a digger after Greek roots and all the articulated parts of speech which make up that glorious language. There was no Greek preposition hidden from him and he could repeat in the original St. Paul's sermon on Mars Hill. But post-war students rightly felt that they would have small use for Greek and so there was little vitality of interest in his classes. He had large feet and it was one of the delights of his students to lighten a heavy lesson by staring at them. A student who was reprimanded for this expressed surprise at Mr. Fetter's sensitiveness and assured him that every one knew it was not his feet but his shoes that were large.

"Is it true, Mr. Fetter," this incorrigible asked with great innocence, "that your feet don't touch your shoes, top, sides, or bottom?"

Colonel William J. Martin, though he taught scientific and hence unalluring subjects, was fairly worshiped by all the students. This was because he had served throughout the war in the Confederate Army and had shown conspicuous gallantry in battle. Looking back, one knows that the quality of his courage was no finer than the moral bravery which the older professors had shown. But we were too young to understand that and besides the roar of the cannon still echoed in our ears. Heroism for us must needs wear a uniform. So we gave our adulation to the soldier of the faculty and it was not wasted, for he deserved it thoroughly. We never nicknamed him; we never knew how.

And last there was Sol. Pool, Adjunct Professor of
Mathematics, who could not quite carry the faith that
was in him to a Q. E. D. He was a small, soft-voiced man
who never measured up to our standards of masculinity.
The boys used to imitate his gentle, meticulous enuncia-
tion in an imaginary speech:

"Young gentlemen, as I came to class this morning, I
saw a frog sitting on a large stone. So I picked up a rock
and I cast it at him. But I missed him. Then I took up
another rock and cast it at him and I hit him just where
I had missed him before!"

Of course there was no truth in us but we swore that
this was Mr. Pool's idea of a great adventure. Well, at
all events, the increasing pressure of poverty and uncer-
tainty was too much for him; he "went over" to the
Federal sympathizers—as we used to put it—and secured
(through his *brother*, a powerful politician and *afterwards Senator*) an appointment as assessor of Federal
taxes. He had several young children and his need was
great; also the temptation to follow his brother down the
easy path must have been great. But youth is unmerci-
ful and we made few excuses for him. The understanding
was that he should finish out his term at the University
but this arrangement was made without consulting the
students. As soon as they knew definitely that the thing
was true, they began a systematic rebellion. Some of the
boys got up early and caught a number of snakes, lizards,
etc., and put them in the empty stove in Mr. Pool's
recitation room. (It was springtime and fortunately no
fires were lighted.) When class began, one of the boys
opened the stove door and immediately the reptiles
crawled out into the room. By such methods, the boys

broke up each succeeding lecture, until the faculty saw
the quality of the opposition and terminated the class.

Across the years I can still hear Old Bunk announcing
sonorously as he entered a class room: "Chronology and
geography are the two eyes of history." And I can hear
our ribald young voices tossing this favorite phrase back
in a sort of litany which never reached his deaf ears.

Strange how the physical *poverty and bareness* of our
college life are all forgotten. Only the realities remain—
the courage, the comradeship, the uncrushable youth.

I read everything I can lay my hands on about the
splendid institution which is today's University of North
Carolina and I am warmly proud of its achievements.
But I fancy that if I went back, I would feel what another,
far more distinguished alumnus has expressed. Hoke
Smith, one time Governor of Georgia and many times
Senator from that commonwealth—yet still the greatest
of his entitlements is "son of Hildreth H. Smith, 'Old
Tige' "—returned to Chapel Hill a few years ago. In
modern fashion he drove his car between suns from Washington through the state of Virginia, two counties deep into
North Carolina, and sat down under the oaks in the campus
as the dusk of evening deepened. A curious passer-by
asked him:

"How do you like things?"

"Not at all," was the Senator's resentful answer. "I
remember Chapel Hill as the loveliest village of the Piedmont. I find it all cluttered up with magnificent buildings!"

Of course, no one would have the magnificent buildings torn down. No one would change this fine university
town back into the lovely village of old. The present
University is a sort of reservoir of knowledge where the
4

clear waters of idealism are protected by the best of all safeguards—science. It is, one may say, a filtration plant which purifies the streams of thought that pass from this central reservoir into the scattered homes of the common-wealth, lessening the danger of intellectual epidemics bred of contaminating bigotry and ignorance. I believe that there are too many Chapel Hill men in the state ever to permit our statute books to be blotted by such legislation as the Anti-Evolution Bill which has recently brought ridicule upon a sister state. No, we could not spare a point of progress in the University's development. But neither could we spare the memory of that crude, sweet Chapel Hill of the barren sixties. For *that* was a high adventure in faith.

Chapter VI

THE UNIVERSITY OF EDINBURGH: NORTH CAROLINA ECHOES IN SCOTLAND

THE desperate efforts toward stability which the state made under the sane and conservative Governor Worth; and which the University made under single-hearted Governor Swain were both destined for defeat. The Reconstruction Act removed all the dykes of tolerance and a great wave of radicalism came out of Washington to overwhelm the states of the late Confederacy. North Carolina was crushed and the University closed its doors in August, 1868.

But even before the final closing of its doors, conditions at the University had grown chaotic and in 1867 my parents concluded that I would be safer if transplanted from such exciting influences. So I was deported to Scotland, to try my hand at a degree at Edinburgh. The choice of Edinburgh was partly dictated by my Scotch ancestry and the associations which my family still had with the old country; but it was also due to the representations of an old schoolmate of mine, Lucius Suthon of Louisiana, who had gone to Edinburgh in 1866 and who reported in his letters the excellence and the inexpensive character of the college course.

In New York I joined Mr. John White and his family, of Warrenton, who were en route to Liverpool, where Mr. White was establishing an import business of products grown in the southern states, cotton, tobacco, and naval stores—all the products of the pine tree, tar, pitch, turpen-

tine, etc. It had been arranged for me to go with them
and their company of friends on what then seemed a long
journey; their proposed residence in England had been
a consideration in selecting Edinburgh as a desirable
place to complete a university course.

Mr. White's family and my own had been closely and
pleasantly associated for many years. Both were of Scotch
ancestry and had been held together by that bond, as
well as by close business associations. Mr. White had
come from Fifeshire as a lad to join his brother who was
a partner in general merchandise with my grandfather
and who, when my grandfather retired from business,
succeeded him and was an unusually successful merchant
when the War came upon us.

On account of the anticipated need for material from
abroad when the Federal blockade began to tighten
around the shores of the South and to make scant our
imports, Governor Vance had appointed Mr. White Commercial Agent for North Carolina, resident in Great
Britain with broad powers to purchase material for the
comfort of the North Carolina soldiers. As a basis of
credit the Governor had bought and shipped to him cotton, naval stores, and other North Carolina products
much in demand at that time in England. Mr. White had
performed his mission with economic and signal success.
He made several voyages at personal hazard and suffered
a serious attack of yellow fever at Halifax, Nova Scotia.
So closely had he purchased that there was even a small
balance to the credit of the state when the extinction of
the Confederacy closed his transactions. The material
thus purchased had been shared by Governor Vance with
other Confederate states, especially those whose limits
were occupied by the Federal troops.

As will be seen, then, the voyage to England was an old story to Mr. White but to me it was an adventurous undertaking. The qualms that I had, as I looked back at the receding shore and at the skyline which in that day was sketched with no violent italics, were not patriotic. I was on my way to a land which could beget that sentiment more readily than this strange, prosperous northland from which I was setting sail. No. My longings were all for those from whom I had parted several days before; for those who sat by the River of Chebar in captivity, south of that invisible but perceptible line which divided what were to me inexplicable northern "isms" from the delightful and courageous bourbonism in which I had been brought up.

After an agreeable voyage of eleven days on the good ship *Nebraska*—ships, even with the name *Nebraska*, are always called good—I saw the green fields of Ireland and the white fences around Queenstown. As we went out of Prince George's Channel up to the marvelous and, it seemed to me, never-ending docks of Liverpool, we passed Birkenhead, the great shipbuilding town where the *Lord Clyde*, afterwards the *Advance*, had been built. It felt homelike to see the home of our great blockade runner.

In Liverpool, I parted from my friends at the famous Adelphi Hotel and set out via the Shakespeare country for Edinburgh. At Carstairs the country, faces, voices, everything changed. I was in Scotland, where my grandfather, whose name I bear, had been born; it was almost a home-coming. In the compartment in which I was riding, were two fellow passengers, a fine looking man and a bonnie lady, his wife. We were getting into the north now and it was growing cold, and as I wore a light cloak,

I began to feel it. (The compartment was heated by a
sort of violin case, a metal container filled with hot water.)
The gentleman got out his flask and after having proffered
it to the lady, asked me if I wanted to warm up a bit. I
poured out a good man's drink and tried to swallow it.
If it had been taken from the lake that burns continually
it could not have seemed hotter to me. It was my first
drink of Scotch whiskey without water. It brought the
tears to my eyes and made me understand why the Scotch
had a burr in their voices.

The friendly Scotchman led me on to talk and evidently
enjoyed my frank dislike of "the Yankees," which I took
no pains to hide from him. On leaving, he told me he was
Sir Robert Anstruther, of Fifeshire, just across the Firth
of Forth, and invited me to what is now called a week-
end, when classes did not hold at the University. It may
be that the unco drap foists sudden friendships; certainly
it unlocked the door of a hospitality that I always found
open.

I got to Edinburgh in the early evening. My first
amazement was the Castle looming above the narrow,
tortuous streets. I had never seen such a feature, half
nature, half art; and have never seen another.

A short drive brought me to my friend's address—
where he had already engaged lodging for me—in a close,
or blocked-off street, forming one side of a small square.
There were a number of boys from the southern states
who had been drawn to Edinburgh by much the same con-
siderations which had influenced me, and Lucius Suthon
immediately introduced me into the colony where a fresh
face from home was assured of welcome. I may add that
there were a few American boys in the University from
states which had not been "lately in rebellion," but it

was not considered particularly necessary to know them, indeed, it was hardly good form.

Next morning, immersed in a raw Scotch mist, I made my way to the University and past the tremendously imposing janitors at the bronze gates into the graceful, balconized quadrangle. These janitors were ex-soldiers who had seen service in the Crimea, in India, and other parts of the overseas dominions. They were of the Black Watch and other Scotch regiments and stuck to their own tartans. Six footers for law and order in a University seemed rather tyrannical to one used to the lax atmosphere of Chapel Hill where a lone constable stood in proper awe of the students.

In the groups of students moving purposefully from class to class, well armed with books—here and there among the groups a woman student too!—I got my first near-up into the Scotch pursuit of learning for learning's sake. Naturally I made comparison always with the University of North Carolina since that was the only college I knew. And in my first day at Edinburgh I saw more serious seekers after knowledge than the population of my home town and Chapel Hill thrown together. Education was a serious matter here, and seriously approached. I had a secret hope that I would be hazed, deviled, or fagged, but on the contrary I was left very much alone with my own reflections.

In making the rounds of the classes in which it was necessary to enroll in order to go up for a degree in the dim future, I found that I was enormously deficient in mathematics and Greek and had to make up my shortcomings in these branches. That led to my falling into the helpful hands of tutors, advanced students in those branches, and like most Scotch students, in sore need of eking out means for porridge and milk.

One of the tutors, John Marshall, was altogether the cleverest student I have known. He was as agreeable as learned, could spin a good Scotch yarn, sing a good Scotch song, or even a Latin one, and brew a particularly mellow Scotch toddy. He became a warm friend of the southern colony whose acquaintance among the Scotch students he enlarged.

Another tutor who became one of us was Christie Benet. He afterwards accompanied the Vance boys on their return to South Carolina and decided to remain in the state. He read law under a distinguished jurist, Judge McGowan, practiced it with success and became a judge of the state's superior court. Too conservative for the agrarian populist influences which in later years swept South Carolina he went out of office, resumed private practice, and later retired. He chose for his hermitage a place of the most surpassing beauty, high up on a bench of mountains in Casher's Valley, overlooking the whole of his adopted state. Here in a cabin of rough-hewn logs, fashioned with his own hands, he looks down upon the squirming workers below him, filching power from the streams and damming up the unwilling waters. Occasionally he sends to the magazines and great weeklies his views on what is passing below. Meantime he has left his fellow citizens a son who does him and them honor and who has sat in the seats of the mighty, a United States senator from the state of South Carolina. From a schoolmaster to a mastership of law, politics, and literature in an alien land was a long, rough road but it has ended on the heights.

It is common knowledge that the Scotch are in no great hurry to make friendships, but when once assumed, they do not shed them without much provocation. Any socially inclined lad such as I was, with the added advantage of being a bit interesting because American-born, would naturally make friendly acquaintance with many sorts of people even among the reserved Scots. These acquaintances were both valuable and improving.

To have listened to the conversation of the great Dr. Guthrie, orator and divine, apostle to ragged boys; and to have been often at the home of Dr. Donaldson, Rector of the Royal High School and later Lord Rector of the University of St. Andrew's, was more than was coming to a raw lad. But the most satisfying social feature of my life in Scotland was the delightful friendship of a family in Fifeshire. It was there that I was made to feel at home and wholly at ease. My happy association with the Key family came about as a corollary of my friendship with the Whites, my late fellow-voyagers. Mrs. Key was the sister of Mr. John White; and when Mr. White's daughter was invited to visit the Keys at Kirkaldy, I was asked to come over the Firth and spend Saturday and Sunday.

They had a beautiful stone house on a hill which commanded a sweeping view of the sea and the hills beyond and was on the edge of the "lang town" of Kirkaldy. All the comforts had been built into the house and the household was of the sort that goes with gentleness. If the older members of the family were a bit reserved, after the manner of their nation, yet the voices of the girls were sweet and gay and there was music in the flying feet of the boys. There was much to entertain the fortunate guest in the household; a trap to drive through the estates

of Rosslyn and the hills of Braehead; long walks leading
to the braes and woods; the privilege of shooting over a
neighboring estate for partridges, rabbits, and pheasants;
music and dancing in moderation.

The head of the family, Mr. John Key (Kay it was pronounced by the working people) was the owner of a great
shipyard at Kinghorn, a seaport of the P. and O. steam-
ers, carriers in the Indian commerce. During the Civil
War when shipowners were reluctant to run the blockade
into the Confederate States and it became necessary for
North Carolina to own her own bottoms, Mr. White had
purchased through Mr. Key the fleetest ship of the Indian
trade, the "Lord Clyde," which, rechristened the "Advance," in honor of North Carolina's war governor,
Zebulon B. Vance, made many a hazardous but successful
trip through the blockade into the port of Wilmington.
Under the command of Captain Crossan, formerly of the
U. S. Navy, but then serving in the Confederacy, the
"Advance" had slipped by the blockade so frequently
that Mr. Key used to call it a "will o' the wisp ship, often
seen but always at a distance."

The kindness of the Key family to a homesick lad
formed the basis of a friendship which has lasted with un-
interrupted sweetness through five succeeding decades.
And in the World War which knit together all English
speaking peoples, whether they dwelt on the north or
south side of the Potomac, on the east or west coast of
the Atlantic Ocean, I had the great happiness of forming
new ties with another generation of the Key family. All
of Mr. Key's descendants could be found at advanced
posts of duty in this last colossal war; it was a sturdy
stock. His grandsons were in the armies; his grand-

daughters drove ambulances in Mesopotamia and walked with Allenby through Jerusalem retaken. The eldest grandson, Sir Robert Hutchison, rose to the command of British armies and came on a special mission to our people in the United States. In years of peace, blessedly restored, he has represented his home town in Parliament at Westminster and has come to Washington City as a delegate to the Interparliamentary Union which met in our capital city during the past year.

But to retrace the years to boyhood associations—

Growing out of my visits to the Key home came invitations to the home of Adam Black, publisher of Sir Walter Scott's books and of the Britannica. He had been Lord Provost of his native city and a member of Parliament but his attachment was to his books. His son and family were gentle people of rare cultivation. His daughter had more vivacity than a well-bred French girl and she looked at all of us young beaux in the most bewildering way. She became Lady Coats, wife of the head of a great manufacturing house. To see dapper little Sir Peter Coats and his wife, apparently much embarrassed by the weight of her heavy silks and her heavier brand-new title, it was hard to realize that he had made a thread which would wrap a baby world or cobweb the Pleiades; and that he had been caught in the act of giving a great park to Paisley, his native town, for the recreation of his own and other mill workers, as well as a free library of wonderful books for the cultivation of the textile workers.

However—this is far afield. One wanders from North Carolina and it is best to follow Sir Peter's cotton thread back to the land which produced it. First, though, I

would pause for a brief chapter on the University of
Edinburgh itself—faculty and student activities as I
knew them—because inevitably the glasses through which
I have looked on at life were altered by this Edinburgh
experience and unless I provide the same glasses for the
one who reads this record, the pictures which follow may
seem out of focus.

Chapter VII

THE UNIVERSITY OF EDINBURGH: SKETCH OF FACULTY AND STUDENTS

BECAUSE they made for me a gauge by which I have perforce measured lesser men throughout life, I set down briefly some of the dimensions of those intellectual giants who belonged to the Edinburgh faculty in the seventies.

John Stuart Blackie had more spiritual acumen than any man into whose face I ever looked. Everything he had ever heard or seen or read had made a permanent lodgment in his mind, subject to his beck. A poet and master of many' living and dead languages, he had a delicious oddity of action and speech that was essentially individual. He was greatly honored throughout the kingdom and was perhaps familiar with more distinguished men and women than any subject of the British throne; but he always acted sincerely in the good Scotch faith that a man was a man for 'a that. He was entirely democratic amongst the aristocrats and a highborn aristocrat amongst us common folk.

Through his affection for his brother who had gone across the sea and had served during the Civil War as a major in a Tennessee regiment of the Confederate Army, he had adopted the group of southern boys into his clan; and his was the first home in which I broke bread in Scotland. I can well remember the wonderful lines of his face, his fine color, and his bounteous flossy gray hair from which Victorian ladies were constantly snipping locks.

His patriotism was not blindfolded. I recall hearing him begin a lecture to a large crowd assembled to celebrate the birthday of Robert Burns with. this sentence: "I know of no more disagreeable person than an untravelled Scot."

Wild resentment was aroused amongst his hearers.

Once he sent a messenger to me to inquire about my persistent absence from the Greek class. I promptly reported and tried to explain that it was not an incurable ailment; but that just then, the season of examinations being on, it was necessary for me to cut his class in order to fatten my knowledge of mathematics which had ever been anæmic. It appeared that mathematics was his own weak point. So without more ado, he raked his pencil across all the absent marks and struck them out.

"We will begin again," he said.

This small anecdote will illustrate the greater flexibility of education in those days, as compared to the standardization of today. Then a college degree was regarded as something more personal than the sum of one's attendance marks.

Sellar was Professor of Humanities, which meant the interpretation of the monotonous hexameters of Virgil and the varying and scintillant odes and satires of Horace. But he was absent, taking the waters at the German baths. Rumor had it that late suppers and Roman banquets had trampled on his digestion. We hoped that this was true on account of the fun we knew he got out of it, and because it had sent us Tommy Harvey.

Among his other accomplishments, Harvey was an Oxford stroke-oar and a boxer who could have stood up with Jem Mace or Corbett. He was a Latinist of latitude and knew how to put down his sight so as not to shoot over the heads of his students.

Once I was called up for recitation and after a dogfall with some lines in one of Horace's peculiarly graceful odes, he asked for the pleasure of my company after class. I went into his den in fear and trembling, but he was not only polite to me, he was cordial.

"What school are you from?" he asked.

"Chapel Hill," I answered pridefully.

"I beg your pardon?" he said in a tone which told me that he had never heard of the place. So I reinforced my statement with the explanation that Chapel Hill was the seat of the University of North Carolina. This did not seem to throw much more light. I never found the Scotch very strong on geography.

"Just so," he said. "Well, I must say they have taught you the anatomy of Latin. But not Latin. Now will you kindly listen?" said he, and proceeded to walk up and down his room, repeating in wonderful scansion the fateful lines. After which he laughed, shook hands and said, "Read Martin's translation of Horace. It will help you. Good day."

That was the last private interview I ever had with Harvey.

The impression of Calderwood on unthoughtful minds was one of impeccability and orthodoxy. He held Dugald Stewart up before us as a menace. There was an uncomfortable threat that you must not only know his lectures but subscribe to them without a saving grace of mental reservation. I still have a sort of sneaking sensation of pretending to be learned in the mere act of recalling his name. Yet his course was not difficult to those who liked such things as Moral Philosophy.

Peter Guthrie Tait. A miracle of energy on the rostrum, and in the open air just a little better golfer, curler, and outdoor upstanding hand in the games on the Meadows or links or college ground than any of the hundreds of men who were proud to belong to his classes.

The first time I remember hearing the word "dynamic" was, appropriately enough, when I bought at a secondhand bookshop opposite the University Tait and Thompson's *Elements of Natural Philosophy*. Tait was a living dynamo—big, burly, driving.

He was impatient to a degree with regulations in the University, one of which required the roll of the class to be called daily.

"Young gentlemen," he would say, "it takes five minutes to call the roll. In a session this would mean ten lecture hours. I shall call the roll just as seldom as permissible, but I'll drop you a hint that few of those who are not eye witnesses to my experiments will go beyond the examination."

He was an ardent Disraelite—which endeared him to the southern colony—and he was keenly interested in college elections.

The story of his work with Sir William Thompson in linking up two worlds by cable and his share of an amazing list of inventions is registered in science. He produced more interest in my mind in what he taught than did any professor under whom I ever sat and I have always looked upon him as one of the greatest figures I have known.

He had an assistant who wore a sealskin vest.

Alexander Campbell Fraser was professor of logic and metaphysics. He looked the part and in his Geneva academic robe he could have passed for John Knox before Knox became a reformer.

His hair was long and wild looking and so were his fingers. When he defined a "notion," he did most of it with his hands, putting the tips of his long fingers on his notes and repeating:

"A notion is a bundle of attributes let down upon an object . . . let down upon an object."

Whereupon all the Simians in his class would facetiously do likewise. Had Blackie been harried after this fashion, there would have been a violent scene, with Blackie flinging himself out of the room muttering, "Asses, asses, wild asses."

Philip Kelland was an Englishman, a Cambridge man, a born mathematician without even a sense of scenery. Asked if he preferred the Highlands to the Lake Country, he replied that the finest sight he had ever seen was looking down High Holborn, London.

Euclid was alphabetical to him. He had a wonderful knack of leading his students along the straight and arid lines of pure mathematics. He used to delight in telling the story of a prodigy who when asked if he had got all the problems in a rather long lesson in geometry, replied by offering to prove any problem in the book which he said he had read through overnight. The professor meant this story for encouragement, but it was really a terror.

He had the manner of a well-bred parson and college scandal about him was so clean that it could have been bandied about in a nunnery. Blackie's last word about him was:

"I was not surprised at the final dismissal of dear old Kelland from his terrestrial service. All winter he was drooping as a flower with a broken stalk. It is pleasant to remember with what a bright flash of geniality he departed."

5

Masson was a complex soul. He was a radical and had gone so far as to edit a Free Kirk paper; yet the demonstrations by his class whenever he appeared would seem to fix him as the most popular professor of his day. He believed in novel experiments like university education for women, a baker's dozen of whom we already had in the University. As far as his kind heart would permit hatred, he hated tyranny.

Frowsy looking and always struggling unsuccessfully with his eyeglasses, yet he was a pleasant person to look at. His voice was deep and had much melody in it.

I have my lean, feeble notes of his lectures on English literature and his lectures are themselves literature. In his great work on *Milton and His Times*, hand-in-glove with Carlyle, he literally resurrected Cromwell and created a new and most powerful Cromwellian spirit in the kingdom, and I fear in the University. Cromwell, after his head had been on top of Westminster for twenty-three years and had then been removed and buried in a place that no man knoweth but which will always be guessed at, was doing very well as he was. But they must take him up, these Scotch irreconcilables, and make him much the vogue.

At one of the usual monthly composition exercises in Masson's class, I recall that he gave out the subject "East Wind." That seemed an easy one at Edinburgh so we all tried our hands at it, but when the man who was adjudged the prize-winner read his essay to the class, I was so ashamed of my unmentioned effort that I resolved on the spot never to be an author and I have kept the promise—until now.

So much for the intellectual side of our college life in Scotland.

Political feeling ran high at the University and the southern colony at once took sides. We had brought all of our unreconstructed likes and dislikes with us and I remember how astonished our Scotch friends were when, in the voting for Lord Rector, we favored Disraeli rather than Carlyle. Why surely all Americans were Liberals, protested the puzzled Scots! And I doubt if we ever made them understand our passionate young gratitude to the British Tories for the very timid sympathy which that party had shown to the Southern States.

As I call the roll of the voluntary young exiles who made up our colony, many happy names rollic through my memory. Arthur Gay, James Taylor Denegre, Amede James and Andre James,—all New Orleans boys; James Hardy of Norfolk; the Summerall lad, son of Chief Justice Summerall of Mississippi. The Vance boys, three in number, from South Carolina and—also from that state—Daniel Tompkins, Carolus Simpson, George Johnstone and Nicholas J. Holmes; Theodore Randall from Florida; John Bass Winder, William Garrett Stone, Garrett Walker, Samuel Jamison, and Samuel Tatum from Louisiana.

Remembering the pleasant association of Chi Phi club life at Chapel Hill, I proposed that our American group acquire a charter (I think it was so called—at any rate, the conventional permit) to launch a chapter at the University of Edinburgh. The proper credentials were forwarded and the chapter formed, embracing in it every member of our colony. This was, I believe, the only foreign chapter of an American Greek-letter society on record. It was a most enjoyable social pivot for us until we graduated and quitted the University. After the last Chi Phi had received his degree, the chapter simply effaced itself. It was a pleasant though transitory experiment in transplanting social customs; and it answered a purpose. But it did not accomplish what I now feel sure would have been a fine thing,—that is to provide a new feature of college life which our Scotch fellow students could have perpetuated, developed, and enjoyed.

It would have been something worth while thus to have shown our appreciation of the good will, the interest and cordiality which those self-restrained young men of the cold, gray capital of the north extended to us. The success of Masonry in Scotland persuades me that the Scotch boys would have entered readily into the spirit of Greek letter societies. And I know of no better gift that we could have brought them than an initiation into the happy youthfulness, the sweet, undemanding friendships of fraternal association. For that was just the sort of thing that most of them needed. They seemed to us almost another race in their capacity for self-denial and their unconquerable will to learn. We were poor enough in this world's goods,—as I have shown, all of us came from the losing side in a disastrous war. But we literally did not know the meaning of the word "poverty" as it was spelled by some of those Edinburgh boys. Many and many of them came to class hungry and cold. Anything to get an education, that Ultima Thule of Scotch ambition. Their lives were barren of beauty and stripped of the gaiety which is youth's divine right.

Think of what we could have offered them, if we had had the sympathetic understanding which is the real meaning of "fraternity!" For they could have afforded to belong to our chapter; our own pocket books were too thin for us to embark on any ambitious undertakings,— to buy or lease a fraternity house, or commit ourselves to any financial obligations. We used to meet in the lodgings of certain members of the chapter and the Edinburgh chapter levied its taxes on affection, not on the purse. So those Scotch boys *could* have belonged, and how I wish we had asked them! But we were a group of homesick boys clinging together, too young for altruism and too naïve for foresight.

Chapter VIII

VACATION DAYS IN PARIS: SPORT, GOSSIP, RIOT, REVOLUTION

THERE were summer sessions at Edinburgh but attendance was not required for a degree, so our American colony scattered during the warm months.

A few of us spent our vacations in Paris, "reading" at the Sorbonne. It was cheap living in Paris, and the French which we assimilated in this entr'act manner was so much added to our winter store of education. Thus—we explained to our distant parents—we could kill two birds with one stone. Of course there is only one live bird; the second one is always a reflection. But Parisian mirrors have a trick of making reflections more charming than reality, and I am glad that I brought home with me memories of the French capital of the Second Empire.

Two of us roomed together in a French flat, seven flights up, belonging to a physician whose clever geniality made all things easy for us save the steps. He was half English, our host; absolutely serious in mind, physically French. He had made the Grand Tour as tutor to a rich Russian and once, by accident, he had been called upon to visit and relieve King Louis Philippe when the king lay ill at his residence in Neuilly. These two services held him bound in a sort of servitude to royalists and to Bourbon habits of thought.

His mother was an antique who used to describe with much animation of body and mind the scene when her nurse had held her up above the heads of the mocking crowd to see her own father's royalist head chopped off. The history always had a fascination for us, because we had not forgotten the realities of the light taking of life.

I did not then but I do now question the accuracy of the story. Yet why? The guillotine was busiest in 1794. This was in 1867 and she described herself as nearly eighty years old. We boys liked her. Her dislike of the Emperor to whom she always referred as *"cochon,"* matched our own antipathy for certain people in authority in our homeland.

The doctor's wife was a type of better-to-do French peasant who had come up to Paris. She was so plain that she flagrantly defied the fashion in paint and powder. Still there was a Gascon of the Hebrew variety who affected shepherd's plaid trousers and was supposed to have a competency, who dangled at her side and could be counted on at a certain bench near the Porte d'Orleans each morning. He always fetched, in a crumpled bag, a limited amount of bon bons for mademoiselle, her daughter,—a very blond, very pretty, flaxen-haired tomboy, aged ten. This child was the best French teacher I ever had. We knew about the same number of words and she expressed herself in the natural, simple sentences that I could comprehend without the hateful process of translation. In the mornings, after our *café au lait*, she and I used to walk in the park, bandying French and ridiculing the Emperor. The flirtation at the bench behind us was very simple, very innocuous, and was merely in imitation of the fashion of the court which must be copied regardless of political prejudices!

The two of us who lived with the doctor were afforded through the kindness of this friendly family two rather amusing glimpses of French life. Once when we were invited for a week-end with the grandparents at Melun, near Fontainebleau, we were accidental spectators at a *battue* which is the French idea of bird shooting. The killing was very awkward and the whirring pheasants and partridges were picked up by the basketful. The North Carolina state of mind revolted at seeing birds driven from cover by men with sticks and murdered by batteries of guns turned loose on them. But that was what wealthy Frenchmen paid for and called "sport." This glimpse of a *battue* gave us an understanding of a story which used to go the rounds, of an Englishman who, on beholding one of these massacres, exclaimed, "Are you going to shoot the bird running on the ground?"

"No, no," replied the Frenchman. "I am going to wait until he stops."

The second shock to our Carolina prejudices was even more severe. Madame had us invited to the home of an artist of distinction where we saw some pretty pictures, heard some wonderful music, and were presented to some colored people! This was quite out of our habit, but the habit of hospitality was strong enough to make us mind our manners, though we learned "How to don't" in future invitations.

The dark events of 1870 were still secrets of the future, but a strong tide of republicanism was even then rising in France and although we were unanalytic observers we could interpret certain dramatic occurrences.

The Grand Prix was the annual excitement to which went the exclusive French world,—all the world, the top guests being the Emperor and Empress. We expected an outburst of enthusiasm upon the royal arrival, but when the Emperor led the way into the royal box a single *viva* gave him welcome; and the answering jeers of the crowd showed the real temper of the people.

Then the race. There was keen division of faith in the two favorites, the English horse Drummer and the French horse, Glaneur. The race was hot. The French horse won and enthusiasm for the victory of the noble animal over his hereditary foe gripped the immense concourse. When the Emperor presented the gold cup to the owner of the winning horse, the crowds surged around the royal box and cheered to fatigue. The news was quickly relayed to Paris and the roads leading to the city were lined with crowds, as were the streets of the capital itself. The royal carriage was cheered to the echo and the Emperor was once again a patriotic symbol, the personification of France—until tomorrow. Tomorrow the fickle populace would resume criticism.

Henri Rochefort, brilliant, aristocratic communist, editor and orator, ridiculed the Emperor unmercifully, accusing him of hiding behind the bustle of his wife when he had her accompany him on a drive through the city. To avoid arrest, Rochefort fled to Belgium, where he had printed thousands of copies of his paper *The Lantern*. The question was to get these papers smuggled into France. His humor equaled his ingenuity; he bought thousands of plaster of paris busts of the Emperor, filled these hollow simulacra with *Lanterns* and sent them with patriotic messages all over France.

In 1869 Paris had an epidemic of uprisings. The son of that mild dictator, General Cavignac, unsuccessful candidate for the presidency against Napoleon III, carried off the high honors at his military school. In order to give distinction to what we would call the final exercises, the Emperor honored the occasion with his presence. When the lad was called forth from his classmates to receive an emblem of the honor he had won, his mother motioned him to retain his seat. He obeyed the gesture, to the great embarrassment of the authorities and audience. It was not only dramatic, but in the eyes of the French it was much worse,—it was awkward. The radical papers made much of the incident.

Following close upon the heels of this incident came another which was more far reaching and which brought into the glare of public attention a new and great figure, the eloquent Gambetta. It was simple enough in its beginning and after this fashion. It was proposed, innocently enough, to put up a statue to Dr. Baudin, a representative in the French Assembly, who had been shot down and killed in the streets when Napoleon seized the government and made himself emperor. The newspapers printed the list of subscribers to this monument. The government prosecuted the newspapers for inciting insurrection. Gambetta defended the newspapers and aroused a mighty spirit of revolt against the Empire. It was a brilliant performance and threw Paris into a delightful frenzy. There were outbreaks all over the city, which were advertised in advance on billboards, much as a circus would be heralded in our country.

Acting upon such advance information of an *émeute*, my comrade and I were hurrying our dinner on one occasion in order to get out and see the excitement. Our host was a little petulant at our bolting a carefully planned meal and gulping good wine at ten cents the bottle.

"Why do you hurry?" he asked, "Riots never begin until eight o'clock. The workmen must first have their dinner."

He knew his people; as he predicted, the riot began on the stroke of the appointed hour. We thought them strange rebels, tense Anglo-Saxons that we were. But I have lived to see America develop much the same light pragmatism in public affairs.

To us it seemed an opera bouffe fight, the riot which we witnessed that night. In a bloodless battle, the cavalry swept the streets clear of people and shortly began the clean-up of hats, coats, canes, women's *chignons*, broken furniture and what-nots which littered the pavements. Everything must be in order for next day's trading and trafficking. This, you perceive, was a French riot. In England or America there would have been a real blood letting; but here it was at most an artistic gesture to let the Emperor know that the French people had grown weary of him and desired a change.

On another occasion my friend and I were favored with a rather private view of the shaky foundation of the Empire. Walking to one of the grand reviews staged periodically on the wonderful oval of the Longchamps, we mistook our route and came out at an unfrequented gate. There we found drawn up a glittering cavalcade. The police stopped us and refused to let us either go forward or return over the road by which we had come. So we waited, willing witnesses to the scene which followed. At last came the Emperor in his state barouche, surrounded by his *cent-garde*, a really wonderful cavalry staff. The little prince was tucked in between two gray mustached warriors for safe keeping. The Emperor's fine Arabian horse, gentle as a kitten, was now led up and the diseased old man was literally lifted into his saddle to canter off to review his troops. The police warned us to keep discreet tongues in our heads but they could not censor the

picture we had seen. Despite our sympathy with the
French people, despite our lack of political acumen, we
were not surprised in the following year when the bull-
dog Prince Bismarck crushed this broken-down royal
roué. The one was blood and iron, the other the melo-
dramatic nephew of his uncle.

From such a falling Empire, ripe for war, with rebellion
already putting finger to nose in insolent gesture, we were
shortly to return to our own land. To the southern states,
where the political tyranny of our conquerors was frus-
trating recovery from past battles and where the fight
for political and social integrity was on in desperate
earnest, that permitted none of the waste motion of
gestures.

Chapter IX

SALEM IN THE EARLY SEVENTIES

HOME again! Though I must confess that I did not immediately appreciate the serious significance of coming home to the monotony of defeat. The pulsation of Liverpool and New York and the rush through the ocean still stimulated me.

New York was immense, bustling, but with somehow an air of transiency; in contrast to the European cities unmistakably new. I stopped at the New York Hotel to which all Southerners seemed to gravitate, possibly because there was a legend that it had been hospitable to them even through the war. While standing in front of this hotel I heard the newsboys crying their papers containing cablegrams of the death of Charles Dickens. Remembering him as I had last seen him on a lecture platform in a great hall in Edinburgh,—rather foppishly dressed and wearing a double watch chain, reading in his charming voice the marvelous scene of Bill Sykes's death—I felt myself caught up into the universal grief at his death.

While I had been away, my family had found it advantageous to move from Warrenton, North Carolina, to Salem, Virginia, and they had sold our old home. Letters awaiting me in New York directed me to collect the purchase price of the old house from Mrs. Gaines (widow of General Gaines and a famous litigant of her day, having cases before the United States Supreme Court for fifty years!) who had bought the place for her daughter. It is amusing now to remember that I carried this money on my person from New York to Salem, Virginia, because in the then state of banking and express service between the sections, personal collection and transportation seemed preferable.

Through Washington and across the Potomac. Into Virginia, filled with battle-scarred landscapes and the empty echoes of destruction. It was raining and wet pines and sweeping clouds capped a dreary scene. At Charlottesville the hills remembered aspiration; and there were groups of students in evidence,—young life and hope. Then Lynchburg, the twin Peaks of Otter, and the beautiful Valley. At Liberty we had a bountiful supper, the very odor of which was appetizing. I met some friends there and they introduced me to the owner of the small hotel, who stood bare-headed, welcoming his guests. He looked a Boniface; he had commanded Stonewall Jackson's brigade and was now brave enough to keep an inn and to feel only pride in his work.

The beautiful blue mountains had literally put their arms around our little home. Our farm—they have farms and not plantations in that section—was situated three miles from Salem, a typical old Dunkard town, with the houses opening directly onto the street, built of brick and with dormer windows. The Roanoke River was the north boundary of our place and the only other farm on our side of the river in the half-moon valley was that of Dr. Baer who came from Middletown near Frederick, Maryland. He and my father had both done much surgical work in the army hospitals during the war—albeit on opposite sides of the battlegrounds—and so they had much in common.

When General Rutherford B. Hayes was wounded very severely it fell to Dr. Baer's lot to have charge of his case.

He was most successful with it and earned the friendship and gratitude of the General. When the latter became President of the United States, he offered Dr. Baer one of the most desirable positions in the state of Virginia, which the doctor declined, understanding well that acceptance of a position of that sort would put him askew with his neighbors; and he valued their cordiality more than the money. His sensitiveness to neighborhood sentiment was the more noteworthy in that he was a Republican. But he had married a thorough-going Democrat of the Maryland post-war sect.

Middleburg, whence the Baers had migrated to Salem, has always been a place of substantial prosperity. And the Baers had brought their prosperity with them. It is a personal tribute to them that we did not envy their more favored circumstances. It was only a cause for a simple wonder on our part that a series of accommodating aunts should depart this life in regular order and should always bequeath to the Baers exactly thirty thousand dollars, never more, never less.

Across the river our "Fort Lewis" neighbors, father and sons—I had almost said daughters too—were all six-footers and their hearts were as large as their frames. They ran largely to twins in the family and even their pets were twin bear cubs which disported themselves in the fountain in front of the broad mansion!

Indeed the whole Salem community ran to twins and to six footers. I do not recall any other community which could boast an equal proportion of either product.

My family was already deep in the neighborhood life. My sister was even engaged in the local effort to uplift the mountaineers. Why is it that lowlanders always feel the urge to lift the dwellers on the heights a bit higher?

Her missionary work was appropriately enough con-
ducted in the Episcopal Sunday School. And I recall that
when she undertook to explain to a group of mountain
children the creation of Eve out of Adam's rib while that
passive gentleman lay sleeping, one of the youngsters
looked her in the eye and gave a long, loud whistle.

"Wh-e-e-w!"

I have read no modernist comment of recent years which
was more effectual than that.

Our new home was of a piece with the temporariness of
things and excessively plain. But it was situated in a
beautiful maple grove immediately at the foot of a mountain, and was flanked by a rapid, noisy stream. My
mother made it a home for us in the sense that only a
mother can, and my father made the housekeeping comfortable to her by introducing a system of water-works—
then almost unknown as belonging to the class of modern
improvements. He did this by boring log lengths, fasten-
ing them together, and with such improvised pipe bringing the water from a spring higher than the house, through
the house, and wasting it into the convenient creek.

It was good to be back with my family who welcomed
me with no suggestion that I was a returned emigré coming back to those who had stood the brunt of Reconstruction days. Only my dog seemed to have misgivings
about my home-keeping proclivities; she would not let me
out of her sight, lest I desert again!

And of course in a short while I did leave. There was
the matter of a living to be earned. A most agreeable
opening offered at Mr. Holcombe's school at Bellevue,
where I could earn my living as a teacher and at the
same time could read law under Mr. Holcombe, a learned

lawyer and a most engaging advocate, whose book on "Equity" was standard.

The management of the school had recently been recast and the principal of the teaching force was Mr. W. R. Abbot, a son of the Chief Clerk of the State Department under Daniel Webster. Mr. Abbot was an accomplished scholar and made the school one of the famous boys' schools of Virginia.

While at Bellevue, I got my practical initiation into politics. I rode in a cavalcade of men to New London Academy, our voting precinct (the place where Patrick Henry made his speech against John Horne for profiteering on the Revolutionary soldiers) and there I cast my first American vote,—for Horace Greeley.

Miss Beecher, a sister of Henry Ward Beecher and of Mrs. Stowe, paid a visit to Bellevue while I was teaching there. She was an aggressive school teacher type; we had difficulty in making the boys keep their manners on straight during her stay. They were never quite certain why she had come and there was a lurking suspicion that she was a chiel among us taking notes for *Uncle Tom's Cabin* up-to-date. But the hostility of the boys was, of course, not reflected in the attitude of her hosts, the Holcombes; and whatever observations she was making must have included a note on the hospitality of that wellbred and busy family. As is often sadly the case with reformers, her ascetic personality obscured the really fine work that she was doing in bettering the condition of women. Few were permitted to know the sorrow that tried her.

In the autumn of 1870, the Holcombes were invited to visit their friends, Mrs. Boyer and Miss Letty Burwell, at Avenel, a beautiful home in Liberty, Virginia—now

Bedford City—to meet General Robert E. Lee and spend the day with him. Happily for me, I was included in the invitation.

It would be impossible for me ever to forget the scene. The General sat out under the oaks, with the family and guests surrounding him. He was cordial and friendly; there was a gentle majesty about him. He had come on horseback and I can remember how deeply he drank of the cool well-water when he first arrived. Somehow his presence seemed more like a "presence" than an everyday person,—this despite his beautiful simplicity. When he left in the late afternoon on his famous Traveller, with his daughter Mildred as his companion, to ride back into the mountains about Lexington, the whole community came out to say farewell. There were many more than a thousand people of every age and station of life. They lined both sides of the road. Not a sound was heard, not a cheer, only a silent waving of hands for "good bye." The sight was so solemn that it made one tremble.

In a few weeks he had gone from the blue mountains into the bluer heavens.

Chapter X

CAMPAIGN OF 1872 IN NORTH CAROLINA

IN the early summer of 1872, when the term of the Belle-vue High School ended, I concluded the double duty of teaching the laws of language and learning the language of law and returned to North Carolina to procure my license and look into opportunities of practicing.

My immediate recreation was the heated political campaign which was then in full swing and in which I could not help being much interested. The Republicans had put forward their contention along most radical lines. A black Negro man had practically dictated the platform, claiming complete civil and social rights; endorsing Holden, who had been removed by impeachment from the governorship; and injecting various isms which had been imported by the carpet-bag element. The most distinguished of the deserters from Democracy, Samuel L. Phillips, had begun the campaign with the opening sentence, "Hitherto, I have not been a Republican."

The Democrats stood stoutly against everything for which the Republicans clamored and we supported our contention with the usual patriotic platitudes. We had named for governor Judge Merrimon, from the mountain country and a life-long rival of Governor Vance, a representative of the Union and war sentiment. In those days there was no place for a *Democrat* on the Democratic ticket.

Judge Merrimon was a ponderous person, addicted to the Websterian style of garment and the Websterian habit of four-hour speeches. Vance had declined the nomination. The offer of it was a gesture but an affectionate gesture. He was then and for a long time afterwards an idol of the combined sentiment which was for the war before it had begun and especially after it came and which never exactly learned when it was over.

There was some difficulty in persuading Judge Merrimon to offer for the governorship but Captain Ashe says in his veracious chronicle of the time that it was "freely said that if he were elected, he would succeed John Pool in the Senate. He only then consented to run." In the present degenerate days and in the simple language of Tammany or of our own North Carolina "machine," this would be considered a "trade," but in those days of profound simplicity it was "anything to beat Grant."

The national features of this election were historically and dramatically set. As North Carolina voted in August, it led the procession and there was keen and nation-wide interest in the result. The Negroes voted for the first time for a president and were drilled to vote early and often. The presidential contest was between the regular Republican party, supporting Grant, and the Liberal Republicans, whose candidate, Horace Greeley, had been endorsed by the Democrats.

An unusual feature of our local campaign was the presence in our district of a trio of mulattoes with a gift for hustings speaking. It was the first time that singing campaign songs had added life and lightness to a serious situation. To this trio was assigned the duty of popularizing the Liberal Republican opposition to the arbitrary power in this Egypt of politics. They were well financed—indeed, their provision in this respect, in view of the scantiness of money at that day, was enough to make us white people gape. And they were so well coached in their manners that they got the good will of all sorts of people. The whites attended their meetings in almost as great numbers as the blacks and they earned their wages in effect. But the regular Republican organization scented the danger and dispatched cabinet officers, the Vice President and some well-known speakers to recapture the ground.

Fred Douglas, the Negro orator, was sent into the denser populations of colored people in the eastern counties. He spoke before a multitude in Warrenton. He was an imposing figure; had a brown complexion and a massive shock of hair; an educated, trained platform manner. His racial instinct to magnify himself and display his superiority made him speak along lines that were so much metaphysics to the audience. They had come to hear pæans of praise for office holders and denunciation of the old masters, with jests broad enough to get over the platform.

John Hyman, a colored barkeeper and later a successful candidate for Congress, had placed on the speaker's table a glass of sherry for Fred Douglas's refreshment. Douglas sipped it between perorations, explaining to his audience that it was not liquor, but sherry wine; and that while it might have been worse, it puzzled him to see how. This gave great offense. His hearers did not believe him; and John Hyman, who had donated the wine, remarked that "Mr. Douglas's manners—what he has— may be good enough for his northern friends but they don't set well with folks who know what manners is."

The regular Republicans followed the military tactics of Grant, their leader, and they sat down to the task of carrying the state in a thoroughly businesslike manner.

The Federal courts were prostituted to their purpose
and issued thousands of orders of arrest for Democrats
who were accused of belonging to the Ku Klux. A quarter of a million dollars was spent on tipstaffs and under-
lings connected with the courts. Every branch of the
Government was called upon to furnish its quota of force.
The Congress had passed bills promising social equality
to the black; every state had its garrison of troops placed
conveniently to suppress any outbreak which should be
kindled by political provocation. The idea of allowing
the possession of the Government to pass out of the
party's hands was not tolerated.

On the other hand, the Liberal Republicans made a
straightforward effort to check the growing arbitrary
power of the Executive. They discussed bravely the cor-
ruptions of the Government, and the character of the
men who mastered the movement was such as to challenge
confidence. They were possessed of ample funds for an
honest campaign and were liberal with them. The Democrats in national convention had unanimously endorsed
the movement, as an earnest of their desire to show the
country that they were still a great national party. But
there was a large and influential element of what might
be called old-fashioned Democrats who refused to commit
themselves to the undertaking. North Carolina had many
Democrats who could not be induced to forego their prejudices against Horace Greeley on account of his lifelong
hostility to the principles of their political faith. As I
have told, my own vote for him was cast in Virginia where
my school-teaching had secured a temporary legal residence.

Greeley was caricatured unmercifully by Nast and
the other great cartoonists and there was a sort of liter-

ary cannibalism in the way in which they devoured one of the members of their own newspaper craft. They ate him up. The result of the election was foregone. The old snow-bearded man was brought into camp and immediately thereafter took his own advice and went "west." He had fought for fifty years for mercy to the under dog.

The sweeping and complete success of the Republicans and the booty of the campaign in the way of continued patronage and the acquiescence of the people in their doctrine of force did not suffice to stave off the economic storm which followed. It seemed as if some convulsion not altogether political was the only thing that could break their hold upon the spirit of the country.

The protest against un-Republican policies and proofs of corruption in every department of the Government, the overbuilding of public improvements, the rehabilitation of two large cities which had been burned (Chicago and Boston), and the friction between the farmers and the railroads shook the belief of the business world in the soundness of the banking resources and with the failure of Jay Cooke, bank after bank tumbled down. In a twelvemonth there were ten thousand business failures in the country. The prices of all money crops fell; there was no cash with which to buy and, of course, there was not much credit. Values of all sorts of crops shriveled up and barter and trade of a generation back took the place of domestic business and of commerce. This was what was called a panic. Its effect was felt in North Carolina, especially in the sections east of Raleigh, whose market towns were the Virginia cities.

It was in such a cheerless atmosphere that I went up for my law license and embarked in the business of taking part in the troubles of others for pay. I know, of course, all the excellent excuses there are for being a lawyer but I could never apply them to myself.

I had concluded reading the prescribed law course under a kinsman, William Eaton, an ex-attorney-general, a conservative Democrat, who had followed his state when there was nothing but war and had been called upon to be one of the commissioners to visit President Johnson in Washington immediately after the war to arrange for a form of government in the state while it was still occupied by the military forces. He was what Judge Pearson called a learned black letter lawyer, an ingenious pleader, the author of a book on pleading, and a book of forms which is still the *vade mecum* of most lawyers in pleadings and conveyances in North Carolina.

His character for strict and truthful statement was so revered by his fellows that it was said of him that he was the best jury lawyer in our courts because the juries could not separate his argument from the facts in spite of what the witnesses might say or the judge intimate was the law.

He was a fine flower of the old, aristocratic tradition. (And the ultimate product of that tradition was often fine enough to make one doubt democracy.) The depth of his conservatism may be gauged by a tale that was current of his candidacy for membership in the legislature. He had an old darky servant, 'Lonzo, who modeled himself upon Mr. Eaton to an amusing degree. One of the townsfolk met 'Lonzo on the street and said to him affably:

"Well, 'Lonzo, I hear Mr. Eaton is running for the legislature."

'Lonzo lowered his voice discreetly.

"Yes, sir," he replied. "Yes, sir, he is. But he doesn't wish anybody to know it, sir."

Mr. Eaton and I walked every day in the groves and talked of the law, but very, very often, of matters of general literature and sometimes of the early history of the state, in both of which I must confess I had a deeper interest. However, I owe it to a friend always generous and affectionate to say that I could not have had a better instructor; and that my failure to absorb more knowledge and love of the law was my own fault and could in no way be made to reflect on his willingness and complete capacity to give instruction.

At the June term of the Supreme Court when I got my license to practice law, I recall that there was a colored man, also up for his license, who knew more law than I did. His name was James E. O'Hara; he had been born in one of the West Indies; afterwards he became a solicitor and Member of Congress.

It was a Republican court but a court of very great ability. They were men learned in the law and, with the exception of the chief justice, were judges of political profit. They could not stand the gaff of adversity.

Judge Edwin G. Reade,—a former Member of Congress, a Confederate States Senator, and the president of a constitutional convention,—took up my examination in the course of which he asked me a singular question.

"How many nails are there in a barn door?"

My answer was that I had seen barn doors without any nails. He assented to this and said:

"You must come from the tobacco section of the state. Doors of that kind are quite common in my county."

Long afterwards, when he had quit the bench and was one of the first financiers of the state, I asked him why he had asked me such a question at random. His reply was that he wished to test my judgment in answering a question that seemed quite apart from the law, and to find out whether I would be misled by it.

Back in Warrenton, practicing law—or, as my young brother said of me, "practicing *at* the law." Life seemed just one long afternoon. The period was sultry with political oppression, and the people of the state still lethargic with defeat. We had lost the hope of the morning hours and we had not yet won through to the security of evening. There was the long, monotonous pull of afternoon to be endured. But we were illogically happy. Somehow we had learned how to be poor. As we were all poor together, there were no sharp points of inequality to jab at a sensitive spirit. Then just as we learned to bear our fate, that peculiar change in the tide of affairs came along and bettered them somewhat.

There had come into the Warrenton community quite a number of people from the North. I cannot remember one who was not a good citizen. But they never became natives until after a probation of a generation and they intermarried very seldom with the original stock. The price of land had become so low that it was possible to buy an estate for very little money and there was an attraction in the word "estate" which persuaded these people that if they could have a comfortable home surrounded by many acres, they could teach the original owners how profit could be made. They did not reckon with the knowledge which the original owners had of the Negro labor and the variety of obstacles to be overcome. Drawing deeds for these purchases of lands, some few wills—because few people died—an occasional counterclaim about property, made up the bulk of what might be called business.

Winslow Homer was a distinguished Northerner who paid a short visit to the village, of course with no thought of residence. Although he had not at that time come into his full honors, he was already widely known. He had come to Warrenton in quest of unusual country life, among an almost foreign folk south of the Potomac. Registered at the hotel, his name meant nothing to the clerk, but his residence in New York did; and in order to inform himself beyond his fellows, the clerk asked him his calling. Mr. Homer modestly laid claim to being an artist.

"Going to open a gallery here?" was the instant query which gave the artist to understand that the community had heard of daguerreotypes and was not, therefore, unfamiliar with artist folk.

Mr. Homer was immensely interested in buzzards,— the useful and graceful scavengers of our countryside, wheeling in the blue sky. He had never before seen any and he suggested with some diffidence that they might be eagles. Upon being told what they were, he quite seriously replied that he had read about them at Braddock's defeat, where they were much in evidence when the great George Washington himself came very near furnishing them food. All of which showed that a great artist from New York could know as little about the everyday ornithology of the South as the South could comprehend of his art.

We had none of the amusements chronicled as such in the news of today, but we had many diversions in the way of picnics, barbecue in season, and dancing in and out of season. The most convivial feature of the life was a round of suppers which turned the winter nights into bright spots. One wonders at the democracy of those post-war dinners, when one remembers that around a table would gather an Irish shoemaker,—a cobbler; a Scotch merchant; another merchant who had come up from a tailor's bench; a banker who had risen from the carpenter's bench; a clerk trained in the palatial New York store of A. T. Stewart and turned farmer; an author of law books; a son of the richest tobacco planter in America; a future governor; and for good measure, a lawyer or two, and if the occasion fell in court week, a judge. There were most appetizing fowls and waffles, and to whet the appetite, if there were need, apple toddy, distilled from a famous horse apple; pipes and golden tobacco. All home-made—even the pipes—not a crumb from beyond the Potomac. But why a cobbler? Because he could repeat, with feeling, any poem of Goldsmith and all his clever play lines. Why the ex-carpenter? Because he had a fund of anecdote about John Minor Botts and other Virginia celebrities. It was a table where talents were on all fours. And the hospitality was perfect because we were all poor.

It became necessary for me to visit Memphis, Tennessee, in order to settle a question of right-of-way over some land which my grandmother had agreed to give through General Forrest to a proposed railroad from Memphis to Birmingham. This gave me an opportunity of meeting General Forrest in a business way. Determination was a part of everything he did but he was not without the smooth arts of a business man,—and the matter was arranged after some delay in the usual unsatisfactory way of compromise. I was particularly interested in seeing the General because I had seen him once before. When I was but six years old, visiting my uncle who lived in Memphis, I had been taken to Forrest's Negro Yard, where my uncle bought of him a colored lad. The entrance to the yard was through a commonplace two-story brick house. In the yard several Negroes were walking about or sitting in chairs. I did not understand things well enough to have any sentiment about it, but they seemed to be interested in us and to be waiting for something—even my small boy eyes could see that.

Forrest's brilliant military career had of course blotted out the ignominy which would have attached to him in his former profession; and in the new life, where there were no Negro traders, he was making good. Which recalls the case of another ex-Negro trader, a man whose granddaughter has of late years married into one of New York's greatest and wealthiest families. This man was one day bemoaning to a company of idlers the terrible desolation which the war had made in all sorts of business; he was in a great state of despair. General Ruger, who commanded that immediate department and who, being on the winning side, was disposed to be rather more optimistic, said to the discouraged one:

"Oh, do not despair. Things will right themselves and very soon you will be doing better at your old business than you did before the unfortunate war began."

"I'll be damned if I will," said the man without hesitation.

"What was your business?" asked the General.

"I was a Negro trader."

The general laughed and said:

"Well, I rather think the bottom has dropped out of that class of business."

It was many a year before General Ruger's prophecy
was fulfilled. But things did begin to pick up a bit in
the middle seventies. The change may best be dated
from 1874, the beginning of the era of our political safety.
The elections of that year showed a tremendous Democratic majority in the national House of Representatives,
in whose hands were the purse strings of the Government.
Hence it was not a vain imagining that there was in sight
the end of mixed schools, civil rights, ballot box control,
and mismanagement through ignorant and sometimes
corrupt office holders.

The state general assembly felt justified in passing an
act calling a constitutional convention in 1875. To carry
out this plan of social salvation it fell to the lot of the
lawyers and editors, who from custom aforetime had a
monopoly of haranguing the people, to take the leading
part. They had rather more leisure to do this than those
people who followed farming or other business.

An event of statewide importance which emphasized the
renewal of political self-consciousness was the celebration
of the Mecklenburg Declaration of Independence. The
North Carolina people accepted the fact and the date of
the Declaration without question; they believed it to be
true because they wanted to believe. It was agreeable to
their self-esteem, painfully bruised these late years; and
it antedated any claim which Virginia might have had to
the honor. The very act of laying claim to that old, original declaration of independence was a new declaration
of independence. To doubt its genuineness became as
heinous as to doubt one of the ten tables of Sinai. (Even
forty years later, the state legislature refused to adopt for
the use of the schools the best history of the state which

had been written because it was not considered sound on the Mecklenburg point.)

Those years brought out some particularly fine specimens of our representative men. They brought to the front again Scales, Ashe, Joe Davis, Tyler Bennett, and others of that ilk. Many others but these first presented themselves. They had all been real soldiers, soldiers who bore on their bodies the scars of close conflict. Respect for their personal characters was so ingrained in the average man that their political opinions were not questioned. They were known to be sincere. Such men were waiting for the great event of the Fourth State Constitutional Convention.

Chapter XI

CONSTITUTIONAL CONVENTION OF 1875

THE Constitutional Convention of 1875 may be likened, not inaptly, to the Mecklenburg Declaration. But the new assertion of independence did not need any Bill of Rights precedent to incorporate the causes of discontent in the hearts of North Carolinians or to catalogue the rights for which they yearned. It was a protest against actual wrongs inflicted; against malicious bonds fastened on a people held in the grip of unrestrained military power. The Resolves were to right wrongs and even those were expressed in moderate tone.

Such was the state of feeling in which the campaign for the convention, when it had once been called by the legislature of 1874-75, began and continued. It was a fair fight between old enemies realigned. The Democrats could now be called Democrats; such qualifying adjectives as Conservative, Union, etc., had disappeared and the party was reasonably unified. The Republicans were reinforced by a body of well-trained black voters, enfranchised ostensibly for freedom's sake, really to keep a standing political army in the southern electorate. Banking on the Negro disposition, the schemers in the Republican party planned to amuse them with baubles. Not even this was necessary. No colored man voted with the sure-enough white man. If he did, he was a son of Belial and an outcast from his color. Be this said to the credit of the Negro.

Something of the make-up of the Constitutional Convention called at this critical time cannot be without in-

terest to those who know of it only through their grand-
fathers. A great occasion was responded to by appro-
priate men; and out of the meeting of occasion and men
came the fourth constitution which the state had had,
the one under which we now live. The Convention was an
aristocracy in which no one could have shame of membership, be he ever so democratic. All had knowledge of the
duties of public office; they were, for the most part, men
recommended by what they had done. The Convention
seems indeed to have been a sort of sum total of past performance and an earnest of future performance. Many of
its members were destined subsequently to hold high
position in public life.

The martial spirit was and is still so strong in us that
the first names to attract attention are those of the men
who had held high military rank.

Roberts, the youngest of our cavalry officers. Tall,
handsome, swarthy, almost Indian; he might have been
Chief of the Tuscaroras. Barringer, a small, well-knit
Presbyterian, who had fought in sixty-six battles and
who had kept in fitness the finest cavalry brigade in
Lee's Army, to say which is to go beyond praise. It was
a brigade fashioned out of the best material of men and
horses by a military artist, himself master of horsemanship
at West Point, a very centaur,—Robert Ransom. Then
there was Clingman, the scientist, lawyer, and senator;
a duelist who looked upon war as an interruption to be
tolerated only because it excused his inordinate courage
and delight in conflict.

There were two ex-senators and a senator-to-be. A
dozen ex-members of the Confederate Congress, and
members-to-be of the National Congress. Quite as many
who had exercised the delicate trust belonging to judges

7

of the highest courts and of the inferior courts. Four
prosecuting officers in the Federal courts. Two former
ministers abroad and a literary consul-general. Two
native collectors of internal revenue. Negroes of education and no education. A carpet-bag writer of agnostic
pamphlets who believed in all the isms except the isms
of the Bible. There was a particularly contentious radical
Negro, a boaster of his mulatto blood. Another as black
as the Duke of Hell's boots, whose newspaper name was
"Archives of Gravity."

The most notable leader of the Republicans in the convention was Richard C. Badger. He had the gift of forceful, wonderfully modulated speech and of severe statement. Justice Edwin G. Reade, who had been President
of the Constitutional Convention of 1866, called his face
and head the handsomest that he had ever seen. He was
impatient of any restraint of opinion and was as dangerous to his friends as to his foes. His satirical mood in
which he was most at home generally vented itself on
pretension and not persons.

The Convention assembled under exciting conditions
and not without depressing forebodings. Its membership
was almost equally divided,—fifty-nine Democrats, fifty-
eight Republicans, and two Independents. The Independents were inclined by association to the Democrats.
In this state of the poll, Governor Graham who had been
elected a delegate from Orange County died suddenly,
which of course diminished the Democratic strength by
one vote. Also there was a contest in Robeson County
where the Republicans had tried to overturn the Democratic victory by herding and voting a large number of
Negro laborers working on railroad construction. Colonel
French, county chairman, telegraphed the condition of

affairs to the chairman of the State Democratic Committee, who fortunately happened to be General William R. Cox, an ex-soldier of the Confederacy and still a soldier every inch of him. His answer was prompt and decisive. "Hold Robeson and save the State." Many years afterwards General Cox, when he was secretary of the United States Senate and when I was in the Financial Office of the Senate, told me that what he really wrote was, "As you love your State, hold Robeson." But the former command caught the public favor and has since become a shibboleth in Democratic politics. Whatever the exact wording of the General's order, the certificate of election was given to the Democrats.

There must always be a serio-comic effect in almost every important gathering and it was not lacking in this. In order to organize, as neither party had a majority, the services of Judge Settle, a justice of the Supreme Court, had to be asked. There was common gossip that because he was of kin to little Davy Reid, the wise ex-senator and ex-governor was not averse to lending him a helping hand. Be that as it may, the Democrats had the good fortune to get acceptable if hostile aid at this juncture of their affairs. Justice Settle had occasional lapses into pronounced political partisanship but he was of high character and though opposed to the calling of the Convention, had great respect for his own reputation in dispensing justice. He wanted to do what was right. The delegates were sworn and proceeded to the difficult task of electing a president. Attempts to effect a choice were futile for several days. Then Dr. Edward Ransom, one of the independent delegates and an advocate of the Convention, decided to fly into the face of proprieties and to vote for himself after the Democrats had thrown their solid vote to him. He did this on the very sensible ground that it was necessary to organize and that his vote was essential.

Having chosen a head and hand, the Convention set itself down to the work for which it had been chosen. The action of Dr. Ransom commended him to the good sense of the people. In the concluding days of the session, on account of his impartial services, the not unusual gift of a service of silver was presented to him by the delegates. This could not escape the gibes of Colonel Isaac Young, a very able and satirical Republican member. He said that while he was a willing contributor to the handsome service and thought it entirely deserved, still he did consider it unfortunate that those who selected it had fallen upon the fatal figure of thirty pieces.

The Fourth Constitutional Convention sat only a month. It had been greatly desired by a majority of the intelligent voters of the state, especially in the eastern counties where there was a large Negro population, a constant menace to good order. Its ordinances (there were thirty, a majority of them enacted unanimously) were acceptable to the people because they provided that mixed schools should be impossible. This gave great comfort to the wage earners who could not afford to send their children to private schools. The Constitution also set up a system of county government which restored the old "courts of the squires." It restored the Commission of the Peace to its respected position and it provided a local government in the hands of those who had a real stake in the soil. It greatly reduced the number of offices and erected safeguards against future tampering with the Constitution. The new Constitution was ratified by a very substantial majority. It was the conservative and peaceful solution of perilous conditions and the year of its ratification was hailed as a jubilee.

Chapter XII

CAMPAIGN OF 1876 IN NORTH CAROLINA

ENCOURAGED by my always-friend, Fabius H. Busbee, I became a candidate for superintendent of public instruction in 1876. Of course we used the newspapers for publicity and wrote innumerable letters to all sorts of friends, pulled all the strings,—except the leading strings. It was an enjoyable, if unfruitful, experience, and gave me an interest in and insight into the memorable campaign of 1876 which I could not otherwise have had.

Warren County favored General Cox for governor and was proceeding along this line but it developed that Governor Vance, who for a time had been dallying with gubernatorial thoughts, had definitely made up his mind to become an active candidate. This settled the matter so far as the governorship was concerned. The bare announcement of his candidacy swept everything before him. He was the favorite North Carolinian. Faithful in war, faithful in peace, and next to the hearts of his countrymen. Common sense and the refined wisdom of older men doubted the expediency of his candicacy, but if he wanted it, then the folks would have no other. Enthusiasm such as I had never seen swept all the convention delegates off their feet.

I had breakfast with General Cox the morning of convention day in his beautiful home in the suburbs of Raleigh. He had taken his disappointment without any bitterness. We still felt that, as a matter of course, we

could make General Cox lieutenant-governor; and that
later, when Vance should go to the United States Senate
(to which he had been elected in 1870 when his seat was
refused him) Cox would become governor. We had not
reckoned on the adroitness of Thomas J. Jarvis, ex-
Speaker of the House of Representatives and Democratic
leader in the carpet-bag legislature of 1868, nor that of
his supporters,—Charles Price, a rising lawyer of great
merit and who was to be Speaker of the House; urbane
John Manning; and the transmontane flying squadron of
Cope Elias. I spoke to Price about the certainty of Cox's
selection as lieutenant-governor. He looked at me for an
instant perfectly straight and then said without any preliminary, "Jarvis will be lieutenant-governor." Well, I
found that he understood the convention much better
than I did for Jarvis was promptly selected.

The general enthusiasm smothered all minor differences
and such little offices as the superintendent of public instruction in which I was personally interested were simply
parceled out by the leaders according to territorial needs
and also, I must admit, according to merit. John Scar-
borough, a patient private soldier, was chosen for this
particular duty.

Nominations made, there began the memorable contest between Vance and Settle.

The struggle fluctuated according to the locality or the
enthusiasm of the occasion. One of the most notable
meetings was at Oxford. It was set for our tier of counties
and a large delegation from Warrenton went in carriages
or on horseback to participate in the occasion. The speaking was in a large grove of spreading oaks in which were
massed several thousand eager people. Bands of amateur
musicians dispensed stirring discord and platoons of red

shirted patriots pressed around the carriage of Governor Vance which was drawn by four white horses. Mr. Settle had preceded him to Oxford. When the hour for the speaking arrived, Vance was being overwhelmed by the plaudits of his followers. Settle made his way in silence to the platform. There was not a single cheer and he was followed only by a sable porter, carrying his books and papers.

Vance opened the debate and was forceful, earnest, eloquent, and witty. Settle's reply was responsive to Vance's statement; and was entirely fearless. Indeed he seemed contemptuous of the hostile and sometimes insolent manner of the crowd.

Vance's rejoinder was more labored but was still very creditable to him. Then, elated by the advantage he had gained, Settle became hectoring in his manner; too obviously conscious of the fact that he had come off with equal honors.

The two men, in the language of the countryside, could be compared to a bull terrier and a game cock. Vance had the strong face and body and the savage desire to tear to pieces. Settle fought with a certain neatness and cleverness, never condescending to frivolity, and not recognizing defeat.

The national campaign soon flared like a borealis. The Republicans had a trained organization, headed by feeble candidates. The Democrats had powerful candidates with their usual loose-jointed, militia-like organization. The Republican platform charged the Democrats with treason and some of the lesser crimes, while the Democrats charged corruption in the Administration and a menace of imperialism. As the campaign progressed, Republican hopes declined and a jeering militancy grew in Democratic ranks. Tilden was a successful idol. He was really the father of what we used to call mugwumpism, because he typified its theories.

Two days after the presidential election of 1876, the country understood that the result was very close and there was engrossing excitement amongst the people as to the outcome. There was no telegraph office in the town of Warrenton and my impatience would not wait for the first mail so I went to the station three miles distant to get such telegraphic crumbs of hope as I could. The information increased in interest and when the train came in from the North, the conductor told me that reports were that the election was so close that the Republicans were sending agents to control the doubtful states and that they believed North Carolina could be counted in for Hayes; that General Kilpatrick, a noted cavalry swashbuckler whose proved capacity for violence had been felt in Raleigh, was even then on the train with a party of men going to Raleigh for that particular purpose.

Telegraphing my friend Fabius Busbee to meet me at the station in Raleigh, I boarded this train. In Raleigh I pointed out General Kilpatrick and his party to Busbee and together we followed them to the Yarborough House where they took rooms, met several prominent Republicans evidently there by appointment, and—to use the threadbare modern phrase—at once went into conference. We communicated this intelligence to the Democratic Committee and when it became understood in the community that Kilpatrick was back for such a purpose as had brought him, it required the firm hand of Mayor Manly to restrain the disposition to violence. Kilpatrick discreetly departed on the next train.

If I may be pardoned for a personal and romantic interlude, I would like to describe another discovery that I made on that vividly remembered ride from Warrenton to Raleigh.

On the coach there was a noticeable family, a handsome mother with several charmingly pretty children, the most attractive of whom was a singularly beautiful young girl. On the following Sunday morning in Raleigh I met this same beautiful girl tripping along to church and learned from my friend, Fab Busbee, that she was the daughter of Peter Hale who had just established the *Observer*. Never had I seen such enthralling eyes. Be sure that I made occasion very promptly to be introduced to her at the home of mutual friends. But it was not until 1879 that Ellen Hale became my wife. In those days courtship was hard labor and required close application. The Hebraic precedent of seven years probation, while not literally applied, was at least imitated.

The inauguration of Governor Vance in January, 1877, was forever fixed in our state history by the epic phrase with which he began his inaugural address,

"There is retribution in history."
That phrase told the whole story and epitomized the victory of the defeated.

The legislature of 1877 was notable because it was to put into operation the new Constitution which the people had just adopted and was to justify the course of the Democrats in making a new order of things. One of its most important acts was in establishing the Department of Agriculture, the first step in legislating for industrial development.

At the meeting of this legislature, I was elected assistant secretary of the senate and with the consent of my law partner and benefactor, William Eaton, I gladly closed my law books and went up to Raleigh. This official position gave me what is now called a "close-up" of the eventful legislature of '77.

In the House there were few men of note. They were *novi homines* in both senses of the word. Charles Price, born and brought up in Warrenton, was chosen speaker; and with the exception of the speaker and Melvin Carter of Buncombe, John Staples of Greensboro, Montford McGehee of Person, Beverly Cobb of Lincoln, Daniel L. Russell, subsequently governor, and Thomas R. Purnell, U. S. District Judge, there were few figures that stand out to the retrospective eye.

In the senate there was more distinction. That body contained such really important men as James L. Robinson, ex-speaker and president *pro tem.*, and future lieutenant-governor; Junius I. Scales, a sound lawyer; Col. Thomas M. Holt, a cotton manufacturer of great wealth for that time and a future governor; John W. Graham and Isaac Dortch, sons of great fathers, worthy of their heritage in talent and character; Octavius Coke, possessed of a stentorian voice and a gift for popular oratory; Thomas D. Johnston, later a Representative in Congress from the Asheville District; and Dr. Yorke, afterwards a candidate for governor,—an independent Democrat who was elected to Congress while on his way to Republicanism. Then there was William H. Moore, a coal black Negro, from New Hanover, a conjure doctor. Think of the wealthiest constituency in the state having such a senator! But that is what Reconstruction meant.

The logical work of the legislature was to select the corps of magistrates under the new Constitution with the least friction. The legislature was really called for the purpose of giving the state a new form of local government. The personnel of the magistrates was a matter of the first importance because in our system the squires, as they were called, came nearest the people. All small litigation and all violations of the criminal law came primarily to them. The office had been greatly desecrated by being open to and filled by ignorant Negroes and it was imperative to elevate it to its old estate.

In education, the reorganization of the State University and the reëstablishment of firm and fitting foundations for the common schools were accomplished. In the light of the generous support given the schools of the present day, what this legislature did may look pitiful, but it was a good beginning.

The establishment of the Department of Agriculture in its breadth of principle and complete equipment would have been an agreeable provision for basic industry in any decade of the state's legislation.

The enlargement of the means for the physical care and comfort of the insane of both races by means of modern hospital treatment and the establishment of separate schools for whites and blacks were great steps forward. The extension of the Western Railroad, which had been recently purchased by the state at public auction across the mountains, forged a vital link in the chain of internal improvements begun under Governor Morehead and now to be completed in the administration of Vance and Jarvis. It was a remarkably constructive legislature but among the useful builders for the state's good who made up its personnel there were of course some drones.

It will not tread on the toes of the living to refer to the quaint and interesting carpet-bagger from the county of old Nat Macon. This man, Thorne by name, was in demeanor every inch a senator. His personal character could have stood up under any questionnaire. But in addition to believing in the absolute equality of men, black and white, he was an infidel and was thus awry with all the prejudices of our people. He was tried by the house of representatives for atheism, with a view to expulsion as being unfit to sit in a North Carolina legislature. A charge of this kind invited a good deal of violent oratory, with strong religious fervor and not unlike the dialogue between Thwackum and Square in Fielding's *Tom Jones*. "Damnable doctrine" was about the mildest term applied. Sticklers for personal rights and freedom of thought had recourse to all the subtleties in defending the accused but their rationalism could never pierce the armor of prejudice.

Then Thorne himself asked in a very mild way that he might be allowed to file in a paragraph a statement of his religious belief. This was consented to. When his statement was read and was discovered to contain such shocking phrases as a "God without body, parts or passions," it was attacked with vitriolic oratory, especially by a comparatively young representative (who, by the way, afterwards became a judge of the Supreme Court) as being the most atrocious blasphemy conceivable. After this young defender of the faith had concluded his Philippic to the great admiration of most of his hearers, Thorne again asked to make a statement.

Explaining the difficulty which he had experienced in putting his religious belief into words, he said that he had happily found in the prayer book of the Episcopal Church an exact expression of his personal thought. And so he had taken the liberty of transcribing certain of the

Thirty-nine Articles of Faith and using them in his own statement of belief.

The consternation among his prosecutors can perhaps be imagined, especially among the orthodox Episcopalians who were militant defenders of the Thirty-nine Articles but just hadn't got around to reading them yet.

Another rather active drone was a long, lean, black, snaky-looking Negro with a high development of animal shrewdness,—the Senator from New Hanover mentioned above.

He had a certain adeptness in memorizing the platitudes of his political party and he could reel them off fairly well to the great enlightenment of his black audiences. He did not write many letters as I found out to my cost. He early marked me, much to my discomfort, as an amiable body who could help him with his letters. He was very free in his confidences and gave me some most astounding information about strictly party and personal affairs, the secrecy of which, of course, I was under bond to observe. One of his favorite enjoyments was to stop me when I was reading a long *pro forma* bill and, strictly within his rights, to request that I would not read so fast or would reread certain passages which he did not exactly understand. When, under the instructions of the president of the senate, I was complying with his request, he would withdraw it, having accomplished the double play of showing his gallery audience what he could do and of having given me a bad quarter of an hour.

When he left the senate he became what is called a conjure doctor (pronounced cunjur) and prospered sufficiently on the ignorance of his patients to maintain a handsome horse and buggy and many other comforts with which his victims had no acquaintance. On one

occasion an unusually ignorant woman believed she had
swallowed a spring lizard and that he could cure her.
That was an easy matter. The next day, after procuring
a small lizard and bringing it along with him, together
with a harmless emetic, he threw her into a spasm of
nausea and by an adroit bit of legerdemain produced the
lizard which he had brought. This almost miraculous
feat added greatly to his prestige and to his pocketbook.
I asked him if he were not ashamed to practice such de-
ceptions. His answer was very frank.

"There was no way to deal with a fool who thought she
had swallowed a lizard but by getting the lizard. I did
it and she was cured. No other doctor could have done
any more."

The personnel of the Supreme Court was all the otherwise complete sweep of the Democrats left of the Republican control in the state. By its own decision con-
struing the State Constitution, this court added two years
to its own tenure of office. They were unwelcome years.
Continuing cases for the sake of fees is a practice as old
as it is bad, but continuing a court for the court's sake,
abashes comment.

In 1878 Chief Justice Pearson died and Governor Vance
appointed William Nathan Harrell Smith in his stead.
Judge Pearson left a name for ability second only to that
of Judge Ruffin in the roll of the State Supreme Court.
He was a teacher of law, a successful practitioner, a
stickler for the exact letter of the law and an authority
on its application to the state's legislative requirements.
He was an aristocrat, eccentric and repellent in his behavior. Morally honest and of high personal character,
in his political conduct his prejudices made him vacillate

and hence he conformed to the iniquities of the alien administration which continued him in his high office.

Judge Smith was by nature and broad education a judge both in mind and body. The elections of '78 added Judge Dillard and Judge Ashe as associate justices and thus the Court became a very strong one. The Democrats were now in control of all three branches of the state government.

Judge Smith had been chief counsel for Governor Holden when he was impeached and thereby had won additional credit for lawyer-like qualities in a new field. It is interesting to recall of him that in 1859, during his first term in the National House of Representatives, he was actually elected Speaker of the House after the longest deadlock over the election of a Speaker known in the history of that body. The honor of presiding over the House was, however, denied Mr. Smith by a parliamentary device. He received the necessary majority but before the vote was announced he was asked by a thrifty Republican member from the hotbed of protection, Philadelphia, who sought him out at his seat on the floor, whether or not he would name a Committee of Ways and Means which would protect the interests of Pennsylvania. He did not know William Nathan Harrell Smith who replied that he would exercise the office without fear, favor, or affection The protectionist thereupon withdrew his vote which had been necessary to Mr. Smith's majority, and the balloting was resumed and went doggedly on until Pennington of New Jersey got the gavel. In the same contest John Sherman, one of the leading candidates, was beaten by his endorsement of Hinton Rowan Helper's book, *The Impending Crisis*, a best seller of its day and a North Carolina product.

In 1881, Judge Dillard wearied of the routine duties of the Court, resigned, and returned to the most agreeable of all employments to him, his law school at Greensboro.

Thomas Ruffin the second was appointed by Governor Jarvis to succeed him. He was less austere in manner and appearance than his father, the great Chief Justice, whose opinions are regarded as authoritative by the Supreme Court of the United States and have been quoted with respect in the halls of Westminster. The second Thomas Ruffin brought with him to the state's highest court the well-known, intrepid, family integrity and also a supply of the subtle sort of clay out of which Adam and the rest of us were made.

The judges of the Supreme Court had their chambers in the Agricultural Building facing the Capitol Square. It was a great privilege to sit in the evening and enjoy their lighter conversations. On one occasion when the discussion had turned on the question of taxes, Judge Ruffin expressed the opinion that direct taxation was the only really fair method of raising public moneys. That led to the consideration of the irritating excise taxes. Judge Ruffin was asked whether, if he had heard that the revenue officers intended to make a raid on the Flat Rock section of Orange County (his native county) to capture illicit stills, he would give information to his friends there or would let matters work themselves out. He had a far-away look in his eyes but a very determined look about his mouth when he said, "I would put my boy Bob on the best horse in my stables and tell him to beat the wind in getting information to the bellwether in the community that the devil was unchained." We all felt with him in this preference for neighborliness as against the strict enforcement of an alien law. There were many nods but no shakes of the head.

The three generations of Ruffins that I have known have possessed the distinguishing characteristics of reckless honesty, simplicity in thought and expression, and a capacity for mastering every detail of the profession of their choice. The law to which they seem to have hereditary inclinations and the science of medicine in which two of them (Dr. Sterling Ruffin and Dr. George M. Ruffin) are now preëminent in our national capital have both been bettered by their talents; others of the family have won success in the operation of industrial works. A forceful clan, of a very high integrity.

Chapter XIII

JOURNALISM IN NORTH CAROLINA: HALE, SAUNDERS, AND THE OBSERVER

IN 1876, Peter Mallett Hale of Fayetteville began, in conjunction with Colonel William L. Saunders, the publication of the *Observer*, at Raleigh, at once establishing that paper on a higher plane of journalism than had ever before been attained by any North Carolina paper. No other instrument had ever been so potent in developing the resources of the state and furthering the advancement of those works of internal improvement which have in more recent years contributed to her prosperity. Particularly may the development of the western part of the state be traced to the untiring efforts of Mr. Hale to secure for the people of that section those adequate facilities of transportation which are the basis of their present activities.

The state was at last facing the east. And the *Observer* was a sort of Muezzin's tower from which prophets of the new order called out to the people, rousing them to meet the day. At once the inspiration and the symbol of Carolina resurgent, this newspaper gave to those who worked with it an opportunity which could not be bettered of observing at first hand the men who filled the state with courage again to lift up its heart.

Understanding this better now than I could then, I know how fortunate I was to have secured the position of city editor on Mr. Hale's paper.

A half century, a good thick half-century at that, stands between us and those blessed people and times. But I shall try to get back through the wall of years and tell how two really big editors, who set to words the story of the state, appeared to those of us who followed them through the day's routine. If possible, too, I should like to retouch the fading faces of those unconsidered crafts-men whose only business was to carry the bricks up a seven-story ladder where they handed them over to "the gintlemen who do all the work."

Peter Hale got his first journalistic experience prior to the Civil War when he had been associated with his father, Edward J. Hale, the leading Whig editor of the state, on the old Fayetteville *Observer*. At the outbreak of the war, he had entered the Confederate Army as a private, but after the early campaigns he was recalled to the paper where he was needed to keep up the spirit which in a later war we learned to call "the morale" of the people. His success in this may be measured by the fact that when Sherman came through Fayetteville he not only burned the newspaper property but put a price on the life of Mr. Hale.

After the war was ended, the Hales joined an interesting southern colony in New York, where they established the publishing firm of E. J. Hale & Sons. This enterprise prospered but Peter Hale could not be happy with a per-sonal success among an alien people; he must be in the center of the struggle which his own people were making. He returned to North Carolina and, with Colonel Saun-ders, established the Raleigh *Observer*.

Here are a few estimates of the *Observer* made by men eminently fitted to weigh its value.

The accomplished Captain Ashe wrote:

As a political writer, he (Mr. Hale) was no less sound and energetic than when seeking the development of our material resources. He was always true to conviction and to principle, and his leadership was largely acknowledged by the press of the State. His style was easy, clear and forcible. He was an omnivorous reader, was classical in his tastes and a fine belles-lettres scholar. So well equipped, and early trained to journalism under the eye of one of the best editors of the older generation, he never failed to elucidate every subject he discussed, and in his argumentation he brought to bear the full armament of his unusual powers.

Writing in the State *Chronicle*, Josephus Daniels had this to say:

It (the *Observer*) was the best paper published in North Carolina in the recollection of the writer. It has had no equal since it passed out of the hands of Mr. Hale. Measuring our words, we may say that it was a Great Paper, and met the needs of the people of the State. It was a right arm of strength to the Democracy. It was vigorous, conservative and aggressive. It advocated Democratic principles and Democratic measures with an ability and vigor that has since characterized no Democratic paper in the State. In this estimate we believe most thinking men will agree.

Joseph P. Caldwell wrote:

The *Observer* was, by all odds, the ablest paper ever published in North Carolina.

John D. Cameron, in the Asheville *Citizen*, said:

Mr. Hale was an industrious worker, a vigorous and scholarly writer, and of large and varied information. It is fair to say that he did not make himself popular with his brethren of the press, nor did he ever become so. Mr. Hale had a very lofty idea of journalism and he was at no pains to conceal his opinions or his feelings as excited by its shortcomings. But all readily recognized his ability and profited by his labors.

Mr. Kingsbury, editor of the Wilmington *Star*, expressed this belief:

We believe that he was the best furnished editor that North Carolina has ever produced.

James Randall, the author of "Maryland, My Maryland," said in the Augusta *Chronicle:*

He was a first-class newspaper man; he wrote with power and ease. He was as fearless as he was powerful. Under the editorial conduct of himself and Colonel W. L. Saunders, the Raleigh *Observer* was justly esteemed one of the best and most influential papers south of Baltimore.

The above conclusions, arrived at by competent judges, on the editorial quality of the *Observer*, have been set forth at length because there is offending reason to believe that our younger literary generation in North Carolina is pitifully ignorant of the traditions it inherits.

Recently, in a national magazine of wide circulation, Mr. Gerald W. Johnson has stated unequivocally that North Carolina's newspaper tradition dates from Joseph P. Caldwell's editorship of the Charlotte *Observer;* and that "Caldwell injected into North Carolina journalism the singular notion that Republicans are as much entitled to a fair hearing as other human beings." As a close friend and associate of Joe Caldwell, I would like to make the denial of these claims which I am sure he would himself deny were he living. Joe Caldwell had the courage to follow in a great editorial tradition but he *followed;* he did not establish it. And the "singular notion that Republicans are as much entitled to a fair hearing as other human beings" had prevailed in the Raleigh *Observer* many years before it was adopted in Charlotte, at a time too when there was bitterer temptation to be intolerant than existed later on.

One of the things Joe Caldwell used to tell the boys in his office was this:

"The truth, in the end, will always prevail."

One hopes that certain of our clever young intelligentsia (whatever that may mean!) will in time outgrow a deplorable slovenliness of thought which at present nullifies the value of their work; that they will cultivate a little intellectual patience so essential if one is to seek the truth. Just now, they seem to have fallen victims to the Ku Kluxish habit of thought. Their pet prejudices chance to differ from the prejudices of the hooded order, but their cocksureness in waving these prejudices about like banners of God's truth is identical with the fanaticism of the devotees of the Fiery Cross.

The iconoclasm of our young intellectuals, of which they are so naively proud, is a pretty cheap product when you compare it with the courageous liberality of men like Mr. Hale and Colonel Saunders.

Both of these men were intense Democrats, but they had got to be by different processes. Mr. Hale had an inborn and perhaps a sentimental sympathy with the weaker brother and he had the clannish instincts that, outside of the Highlands of Scotland, are not quite so fine elsewhere as on the pineclad banks of Cross Creek. By preference, then, the people who had been beaten were his people. A Whig by education, by grace of the unnatural rigors of reconstruction he was forced into the opposition which became Democracy. But the literal fire and sword of Sherman did not sear from his disposition some toleration for certain Republicans of the cleverer and pleasanter sort, and he could be good company on occasion with such accomplished past-masters in politics as Colonel Ike Young, Governor Holden, Albion Tourgee, John Nichols, Colonel Shaffer, and the great and only Colonel Loge Harris, whose clever articles in the New York *Times* (then

the ablest of the Republican papers) Mr. Hale frequently
quoted in full. There was a grand constellation of Republican planets in those days. If they had talents—and
hadn't they?—if they had lives worth reading or stories
worth telling, and kindliness, the latch string of the copy
room hung out to them. And what shall be said of their
feelings toward him? They all called him Mr. Hale when
addressing him; when speaking of him it was "Peter
Hale" always. Doesn't that tell the story? Is there much
softness or magnetism in the love for the man who is
never known by his Christian name?

There was surely a charity in his politics, and he dif-
ferentiated between the doctrine and the doctrinaire. The
one he knew was hostile, the other he believed could be
friendly.

In personal appearance Mr. Hale was striking looking,
very like the portraits of Hawthorne. The suggestion of
the poetic in his nature was manifested in his attire. He
wore his fine silken hair almost to his shoulders, and his
complexion was as fresh and pink as a schoolgirl's. No one
ever saw him with a beard a day old, and his neatness
was grateful. He had very dark brown eyes. They literally glowed in strong feeling and laughed in humor. When
he was resisting your contention and steeling himself
against yielding, the light seemed to retire into his eyes
and produced the effect of blindness. So that the quick men
around him would say among themselves, "Something is
wrong; there is the blind look in the Major's eyes." He
had large bones and a massive frame and was very tall—
over six feet, though a stoop in the neck from bending
constantly over his work concealed his height very appre-
ciably. This is the picture in my mind of the man who

could be editor, critic, foreman, compositor, manager of big daily papers, and who was.

It is no disparagement to any one to say that on occasion his work could be done by Mr. Hale better than he could do it himself. I have seen him stride into the office at day dawn and unlock, upset, and rearrange the whole outside of the paper because it was not well balanced to his keen, tasteful eye; and he would set up a headline or a display advertisement, never in petulance or temper, but with a kind, "Don't you think this would be better?" sort of way that would simply stupefy the average printer. It gave him great prestige in the work shop and insured a model paper in appearance, as well as an excellent tone in matter. Mr. Hale did not think it was possible to print a paper that was too good for his subscribers, and he regarded a subscriber in the light of a personal friend.

He had at the bottom of his mind some theory like this,—that if the material condition of the people could be made as good as possible, they would be happy, and they would govern themselves in a satisfactory manner. Colonel Saunders acted on the belief that if the Government were kept along simple lines and approved for its justice and economy by the people, then the development of the country would come along in due course through individual effort; and he was not at all impatient about it. In this difference, one can perceive the early party training of the two men. Mr. Hale's thoughts and aims turned at once to the development of the state, and to the day of his death he wrote and contrived to this end. His faith that the completion of the Western North Carolina Railroad would do away with the jealousies between the east and the west has been justified. It

is quite impossible to make plain to those of today how
strong the antagonisms once were, but is not the harmony
of an undivided North Carolina sentiment a result worth
work for a lifetime?

As a party man, he was liberal, and he was by nature
in sympathy with the man with a grievance, even if it
were not too well founded—as was sometimes the case—
but his personal attachments were so strong that they
led him into oppositions within the party. This was
notably so in the famous Vance-Merrimon contest. Mr.
Hale thought that Governor Vance had not given his
paper the recognition that its services and their old-time
relations entitled him to; and besides he was greatly attached to Colonel Fuller, Senator Merrimon's law partner and manager, for whom he felt a deep and reciprocated
affection dating from boyhood. Moreover, he construed
the policy of the governor's following as to instructions
by county conventions to legislators in the election of
senators as outside of party authority and unfair; he resented it. Colonel Saunders did not concur in this view,
but difference of opinion occasioned no breach of any
sort between them. It did lead, however, to the printing of some very able articles on both sides. The fact
that Mr. Richard Battle, Captain Ashe, General Clingman, Armistead Jones, and men of that mettle wrote
them shows what a royal battle it was. No one was
denied a hearing if he had not scandalous matter, but a
good deal of ill feeling might have "died a-bornin' " if
real names had been attached instead of fictitious ones.
Somehow or other, Bill Black will say more insulting
things over the Latin name of Erebus than over his good,
honest English one.

Much the same internal political war was flagrant in
the Shotwell-Schenck controversy, when the whole Ku
Klux business was threshed over and much that was
written had to be refused, and much that was printed
really was lacking in proper respect for the Supreme Court
which was then being tried for its decision in the Driver
case. But the people took a hand in the matter and decided it in the long run in favor of both Chief Justice
Smith and Judge Schenck, who were made to serve as
unwilling leaders around whom grouped enthusiastic followers in this strictly family jar.

The mud cut boom aroused Mr. Hale and Colonel
Saunders profoundly. It struck first straight at a policy
of the paper that was considered vital to the state's best
interests, because it was calculated at least to retard the
completion of the road and to disappoint the hopes of the
mountains. It is drawing too fine a point to say that its
authors intended creating discontent that would force
the state to sell the road to those who would build it;
that would be to discredit the motives they avowed.
But that was the result of it; and the editors of the *Observer* lived to see that great captain of internal improvements, Colonel Andrews, build the road and make it a
part not only of a great East and West line but of a great
North and South system as well.

As printer to the state, Mr. Hale dignified the office
by standing for its deserts. He looked upon his commission as a memorial that he was to repay by watch-
fulness over the public interest, attention, good taste,
and the experience he had gained in the publication of
many standard books. He distinctly elevated the art of
printing in the state and the public estimate of those who
live by the art.

Upon this and the development of Western North Carolina, imperishable results physically and morally, must rest his growing recognition. There was so much about the man that appealed to one's heart, his gentleness and diffidence of manner,—it warns one to desist. It may be said of him and of Colonel Saunders that while neither practiced the follies of false piety, they were born, bred, and died Christians and in a most intimate intercourse with them I never heard an unclean word fall from their lips. They were gentlemen to the manner born.

If I were called upon to say who was the hardest worker I ever knew, I would say Mr. Peter Hale. After seeing if he could not do another's work, he would buckle down to his own and he could do more of it and of a higher quality than anybody else.

But why refuse to face the end of all this? The legislature elected in 1878 was what is sometimes called a reform legislature. Demagogues delight in praising a certain rigorous kind of paring of necessary expenses which is anything but economy. Under malign influence it passed a printing law which hurt only the printer. The *Observer* had relied on a renewal of the law as it stood.

The profits of the printing were to go to the paper. It is but fair to say that for reasons that were entirely proper and satisfactory Colonel Saunders had put very little money in the enterprise and with his translation to the secretaryship of state, his connection with the paper ceased. Mr. Hale had thus to bear the entire burden. He had spent all of his own money and he declined to involve further the kind offers of substantial assistance. Under the advice of his counsel, he made an assignment for the benefit of his creditors. When I carried the paper to the clerk's office it seemed to me as heavy as lead. It carried with it so much splendid labor and so many high hopes; but the end had come and there was only to meet it in a manful way. Mr. Hale did this to the end of his finger tips.

Looking back over what now seems a dream, I wonder at the company of men, nearly all with military titles won by devotion, laboring in the highest and lowest departments of an exacting and never-ending business with cheerfulness and unselfishness; then going down to another defeat with another cheerfulness and a determination to begin the fight over again on the morrow. It makes me recall an inscription on the monument of one of the Dukes of Devonshire, which read somewhat after this manner:

> What we spent, we had,
> What we had, we lost,
> What we gave, we have.

Chapter XIV

COLONEL WILLIAM LAWRENCE SAUNDERS: KLANSMAN, EDITOR, AND CITIZEN

WILLIAM LAWRENCE SAUNDERS was a Democrat by birth; and by mental construction could have been nothing else. An aristocrat from the Gloucester settlement in Virginia, his forbears, like all their fellow colonists, were revolutionists and patriots. They were and are today radical. When they lost their respect and love for the King, they became Democrats forever. They were sincerely and really for the people. Kindly as a woman who has known sorrow, he recognized the divisions in the life he came into and he was not at war with them. He looked philosophically at the storm of war as it came over the land and prepared himself as methodically and as complacently as he had for his first professional life—the law.

Exchanging a captain's bars for a colonel's stars only meant a larger field for his military abilities in service of his state and it did not elate him. He neither worried nor murmured under his wounds. He knew that devastation followed war, as he knew that blind passion preceded it; and he set to work to protect the victims from the vultures.

He was said to be the emperor of the Invisible Empire, as the Ku Klux Klan was known in North Carolina, one of the most wonderful organizations that the busy world has forgot. Born in the unutterable confusion that fell upon the insurrectionary states when the large garrisons of troops which had maintained some semblance of order were withdrawn, it had the purpose to check and cope with the secret Union League by means of which the scum of the receding armies had banded together the credulous blacks in sworn hostility to their former friends, and had robbed them for this injury they did them of the first money they had ever handled as free folks.

The Empire's rites were read in the light of arson's torches and the grotesque and silly ritual could not have bound men together unless it had been in the presence of impending servile insurrection or for the protection of women and children, instead of for benefit of each other. Colonel Saunders distinguished a riot from an insurrection and he knew that the latter had to be fought to the death at the first pass. Will we ever know the infinite woes this organization warded off?

The danger over, however, the Empire should have dissolved like the real armies of the republic when war with the mother country was concluded. But the evil that is inbred in all secret societies, not benevolent, worked in this and there were of course sporadic abuses for personal revenge. The Radical party was quick to seize on this unhappy consequence and having begun secret orders for selfish purposes such as the intimidation of the old electorate—what was left of it—now grew painfully sensitive over a few lashes administered to more or less guilty backs. The darker the hue of the back, the more horrible were the convulsions that were cast. Was it unlike the incident of the young robber in Edmond About's *King of the Mountains* who, when his band was sacking a sleeping village, took a baby deserted in the terror of flight and hurled it into a blazing cottage to destroy all traces of the night's raid; yet who was inexpressibly shocked the next day, while enjoying a hearty meal stolen from the destroyed village, to find that he was eating meat on Friday?

But the time for punishment had come and many men of consequence in all the ways of life were harried and haled to those high in the halls; and with them came Colonel Saunders. He proved a most obdurate, hostile and silent witness of his vows. Nothing of favor or fear moved him to say more than that he was advised by counsel that his answers might tend to incriminate him, and these unchanging words he repeated over and over with a stolidity that did not conceal his pride in his alleged associates. In the bitterness of spirit of those days speedy judgment has, it is to be feared, done injustice to some unwilling actors in that savage drama. None wanted to be witnesses against themselves. But some, incensed at the enormity of the few, forgot on the instant the animus that led them into the order and the good it did and in shame said more than they should. Others, acting in genuine unselfishness, thought that it would be for the happiness of their neighbors and themselves to have done with the order forever; they chose the odium attaching to "State's evidence," in the hope and faith of final justification. But you will see that in order to justify them we have to reason. For Bill Saunders, Bluff Bill Saunders, men of all shades of belief on this still vexed subject,—this phantom and nightmare that guided and misguided and oppressed and perhaps saved us—do *not* care to have more than one opinion. He was a grand, heroic figure.

In Colonel Bingham's Latin Grammar is a sentence describing Ægesilaus as lame in the feet, and Colonel Saunders always reminded me of this great Grecian in physical appearance. He was a large, stout, florid man with small bones. His eyes, very round, were prominent and of light bluish-gray color. His massive jaw conquered agony and was as fine as Bismarck's. When he was suppressing his pent-up fire he had a habit of inhaling the surrounding air to cool his temper, displaying when he did so the cruel bullet furrows, and when he was perplexed and was winnowing a subject, he whistled softly. His naturally violent temper was never loosed against the weak. It was loosed against no one unless his judgment willed it. So anxious was he to do his part that when locomotion became irksome to him he had a room in the *Observer* Building fitted up for a chamber so that he could be at his work. But the ravages of disease were so furious at this time that he had to go to the baths and he was but little in the office proper from my first summer until, on the death of his much-loved former partner and brother-in-law, Major Engelhard, he succeeded the latter as Secretary of State.

I shall never forget an editorial which I wrote on a subject that is a matter of indifference now but which at the time seemed to me to be of moment. The editorial was written in an ironical vein and to my mind was very savage. I read it to him for suggestion. He seemed to relish it immensely and chuckled just at what seemed to me to be the proper places to show appreciation and enjoyment. When I had finished he took the copy and said, with a faraway look, which I did not just then comprehend in its full force, that he wanted to keep that to show to some friends. He kept it and I have never seen it since, but a good long while afterward he remarked to me, in the course of one of our long sittings, that while ironical writing was very enjoyable, he feared our North Carolina reading public was much too serious and too apt to take it literally. It is not an extravagant statement to say that a great light dawned on me about this time, and I tried to walk in its path for many days.

He was a most entertaining conversationalist and his English was as simple as if he had studied the Bible exclusively as his model of expression. He seldom used a big word.

He was fond of illustrating the meaninglessness of all the "logomachy," as the country people call it, and the gush about reconciliation, the blue and the gray, etc., by reciting an incident that occurred at Charleston, South Carolina, when the crack Boston company visited that city not long after the war. In the Boston company was an officer who had been a college mate at Harvard of an officer in the Charleston Blues. After all the speech-making was through and when these two chums had retired to the Charlestonian's residence, to smoke a farewell cigar, the Boston man asked his Charleston friend to tell him in very truth if the fire-eating South Carolinians were in earnest in all their professions of good will.

"Hush," the Charlestonian cautioned him. "We are just as much in earnest as you Boston Yankees are."

Colonel Saunders's love for his state was intense. I really believe that he thought the governorship of North Carolina the greatest office on earth. Above all things he resented anything like dictation from Washington and especially from the North Carolina delegation in Washington about state affairs, and his attitude toward the delegation while personally as kind as could be, politically was little better than armed neutrality.

His was a great power in politics. He somehow by his very silence invited the confidence of men. The leaders, especially the young leaders, came to consult him like

9

pilgrims, and he knew their ambitions and aims. Very little cared he for place but he valued power. While in name the senate's clerk, he was in fact the friend of the court. A mere secretary to the Board of University Trustees, he was more than any one its guardian. If asked to name his greatest work as an editor, I would say it was the Constitutional Convention of 1875. His great permanent work, the *Colonial Records*, again connected the two editors of the *Observer*, this time as editor and printer working together in harmony on a subject dear to them and which they saw grow into volumes which for intrinsic value and for beauty of book-making art are recognized as great books.

Chapter XV

AT WORK ON THE OBSERVER: MURDER, SCOOPS, SKETCH OF STAFF

IT is very pleasant to see grow out of the air just in front of me, full size—and that was pretty large—the semblance of Captain Dick Saunders, the business manager of the *Observer*. I had known Captain R. B. Saunders when he kept one of the finest drug stores in the state at Chapel Hill. No amount of evidence, written or oral, could shake my belief that nobody ever made exactly such peach ice soda as he made, and this will be vouched for by all the belles, and they *were* belles, on the Hill. His receipt for smoking tobacco would make the Kings of the royal weed rich beyond the dreams of a millionaire's avarice. Tests: Classes of '65, '66, '67, and '68. But when the University closed, the drug store went down with it; and Captain Saunders, with his good wife, a daughter of Governor Brandon of Mississippi, set to work to bring up their little ones near Raleigh.

Captain Saunders was at heart an optimist, but in speech a radical pessimist and the comfort I got from him when I was a "cub" on the paper is not worth the lead in writing it. But it did not take a mallet to get into my head that his writings on the subject of the first importance to a million of our people,—how to enrich their land (he was a good practical chemist)—and his stories of our country fairs made him a most valuable man in a newspaper office.

Before I had learned to correct a proof I was sent off one day on just sufficient notice to run for a train. Running was the quickest transportation in those days when it took Ed Lane with four stout grays a half hour to pull the Yarborough House omnibus from the old central depot to Fayetteville street. I went without a change of raiment to Goldsboro, near which a most atrocious murder had been committed. I wasn't the murder man, but he was out and I had to go. Captain Saunders had told me that the right man was never in his place but the man who would do always was. At that time it went into one ear and came out at the other but later it came back through the other ear and stayed there. In due course the train and I got to Goldsboro but I found the whole subject stale. The ground had been preëmpted by Dick Fulghum of the *News*. Is it necessary to explain that the *News* was the other paper, with the accent acute on "other"?

Fulghum knew every man, woman, and child in and around Goldsboro or they knew him, which was worse for me. They had every one been to him and told him all about it—lots more than they knew; and he had copious memoranda of what had not been told him. He had stories that would have shriveled up the New York *Evening Journal*, and I had only the acquaintance of a few choice spirits like Isaac and Hab Dortch, Arnold and Frank Borden, Abe Smedes and the Dewey boys and a few others who didn't take any interest in a low-down murder and were all out of town to boot. So I diffidently suggested to Dick Fulghum that I would go out to the scene and scuffle around the best I could with the murderer and the murderee.

"Holy Moses, no! Let's get some supper and then I will show you the jail and you can have all my notes and write your own account of it. I'll show you where we can get a bully supper."

In these days of scoops, think of that! That man's heart had grown so big, it had shoved out all the little mean things that stick in the crevices!

"Are you going to illustrate your story?" he asked with a little hesitation. I assured him that I could not draw a straight line if he gave me the points. He looked pleased. Next morning, when I bought the "other" paper and the *Observer*, there, in the other paper, stood a diagram of the scene of the murder,—so far as I knew, it was the first illustration of the sort in North Carolina journalism— and though done with rule, if the vulgar understand what rules are, it made my columns look flat, dreary, newsless, uninteresting and unsuggestive.

The same mail brought me orders to write up Goldsboro. I was not the town-writing man but he was out of place and I would do. So I did it. Dick Fulghum was curious as to why I dallied by the waters of the Neuse at the cross of the iron ways, but I had to get even on the diagram, and so I just white-lied it about getting subscriptions and one thing and another until I got my work done and then I stayed over a day to deliver the papers. On the strength of the town write-up and local pride, I got quite a few subscriptions and advertisements,—of course I wasn't the subscription man nor yet in the advertising department but the office had said I "would do."

Well, I got back Saturday night and Fulghum, who went up on the same train, was very generous about the Goldsboro write-up, saying that as it was about his town, he was going to reprint it. I felt that he wanted to think well of it because I was new at the bellows, but all the same his kindness helped me up the steps of the office. When I got in, Captain Dick took his pipe out of his mouth,—a long-stemmed, reed root, Powhatan pipe,— and said, "Hello! Back?"

I knew right then that I had left out a diagram of Goldsboro.

Then I thought I wouldn't turn over the money to spite him, but would keep it for one of the big chiefs; but my anxiety to know how my work stood in the office chewed the bark off that idea and I threw down a wad of money and the subscription form book.

"Bill and Mr. Hale have been talking about you," he said, with all the Delphic irritation possible. I knew it. I had felt it. How could any one not consumed with literary egoism expect the public to understand any un-diagrammed thing?

Just then the familiar thump of Mr. Hale's cane came rapidly up the stairs and as he came in he gave me a hearty shake of the hand and a little satisfied laugh.

"Bill and I have talked it over and we want you to take Woodson's place," he told me.

Having no diagram to go by, I just said, "When?"

"In the morning. Write the announcement now."

That was the way I broke into the *Observer* staff, suc-ceeding Ned Woodson, of Warren, whose sudden and un-timely death had left a vacancy. And thus I can intro-duce myself into this picture of the old *Observer* as local or city editor.

A very important man on the paper, of whom I stood in some awe because he seemed to know so much about a paper and *did* know it too, was the foreman, Harry

Roberts; and next to him was J. C. Birdsong of whom I stood in no awe whatever. He was just a plain, long, lank, typical Reb; an old-fashioned printer with all their virtues and none of their vices. He could work sixteen long hours a day and when he wanted a good rest, he sat down and dreamt about Billy Mahone and the Twelfth Regiment, and wished for a return of those good old days when the shooting was so good down in the Peninsula. His religion doubtless saved him, but it never reconstructed him.

Jewett Cosby was clerk and cashier. He had been handed down some way from the *Sentinel* and was ranked as a veteran. My contact with him was largely confined to those Saturday afternoon matinées when the funds were divided. He was even and rotund in mind and body and earned and kept the good will of the paper and public until he balanced his books for the last time.

Among the regular printers were Charles Kennedy and John McKay, who came from the Fayetteville *Observer,* where they had grown up from apprentice devils to the case. When Mr. Hale came to Raleigh to establish the *Observer,* they asked no questions and made no contracts, but simply walked in, took a case, and began distributing, much as if the old *Observer* had been got out the day previous. Capable, careful, intelligent, sober men, they had a stake in the paper superior to any recognized by the law.

There was Bill Walton, a singularly handsome lad who had stood on a soap box to set type on the Wilmington *Journal* under Engelhard and Saunders and who educated himself in spite of himself to a critical knowledge of the newspaper craft that few attain. He became, in later years, presiding genius in the make-up of the great Washington *Post.*

Another of the old *Observer* men who afterwards went
to the national capital and who became president of
the Typographical Union, in Washington, was William
Brockwell.

Unobtrusive James Pool was one of our regular men
and just one of those valuable men never in the way,
never out of the way, and always the same way.

It would be hard to forget Bert Royster. He was of that
family that has made and makes such an essential part
of Raleigh's life and growth and worth. It is not telling
tales out of school to say that Bert lost no time after pay
hour in beginning to spend his money and in getting in
Tam O'Shanter's best mood. But he was so kindly that
it did not seem to do anybody any harm, not even himself. He delighted then in telling you how much he liked
you and about fighting the Yankees. They were surely
agreeable topics and he never reversed them.

Before telephones and speaking tubes and such modern
nuisances were sent as plagues on the people of the fourth
estate, the devil was a very important link in a newspaper
office. He was the purveyor of copy from the editorial
rooms; and when you went to hunt and wake him up, he
would help you bring back proofs. He always knew what
cases were empty because their geniuses were "remembering their misery no more" and in sweeping up the office
he gathered scraps of yet other information about men
and things that made him a most desirable person to
keep an eye on. He lived in the hope that he might one
day become a tramp printer and blow into New York or
San Francisco on a late cross tie; but he was pursued by
the harrowing and morbid fear that he might in the course
of his indulgence in unnecessary work degenerate into an
editor.

I will reverse the order of our brace of devils, because a line will tell that Dan Riggan was a good looking lad of spirit and sufficient sense to take care of himself as well in the world as in the composing room, and there is every reason to believe that he has done so and, of course, all the hopes are that way. A *gem* on the going away of Upchurch is the only name to give the few lines which Mr. Hale wrote of him. I doubt if you can find his name elsewhere than in that paper. But it is there to stay. He was called Goose Upchurch, why, nobody knew. He had sense and of a rare sort. Before he fell ill, he had sense enough to leave off his evil ways and to go to that sweet tempered Christian pastor, the late Rev. Doctor Norman, and ask to go into his fold. Dr. Norman had a very small meeting house in a very humble part of the city, and I suppose there must have been a score of us there to keep the lad company until "the form was locked up" for the last time, but I do not believe it has been given to any of us to forget the tender modesty with which the handsome young preacher told the homely life story of that poor boy.

The world goes on and some of us with it. A half century back, impersonal journalism in North Carolina was a doctrine not to be tolerated—perhaps it is not today by some half million worthy people—and one who practiced it was liable to the pains and penalties of personal disapproval. But none of these things much concerned Major W. A. Hearne, an editorial writer of vigor and an industrious and intelligent compiler of newspaper matter. The series of articles which he wrote under Mr. Hale's supervision on the development of the state's resources by means of transportation routes have permanent value. The work gave him great satisfaction because he really loved the state,—he said to me once that he had written much against statesmen but never a line against the state. If he had gone to a great heartless metropolis like Chicago, he would have won fame by his felicitous phrases, but he would have died of homesickness. He knew nothing about business beyond securing money for his present wants; and he could never understand why he should not have opinions of his own, and yet express the opinions of others when employed by them to do so.

Another familiar figure in the office was the stocky, sturdy John Bull form of John Spellman. As a long hand reporter and a careful proofreader, he had few equals. Like Major Hearne, he was a man without a party. There was really no Republican paper at the capital to hire them and they had to stand in the market place until a press of work or special work came along to them at whatsoever was right. They were too old to learn new tricks and doubtless felt at election times like a North Carolina Republican leader who once said in an undertone, when the wires were loaded with returns favorable to Judge Buxton,—"I'm damnably afraid my man is elected."

Of quite another kidney was John Syme. With the exception of a few newspaper men with whom he was thrown, I doubt if John Syme was acquainted with a Republican. He was born to the royal ink and had been trained by his father, an old-fashioned editor, whose editorials opened up at 212 degrees F. and got hotter as he warmed to his subject.

William Plummer Batchelor was the *fidus Achates* of Peter Hale and Bill Saunders. His work was always excellent and his presence cheerfulness itself. If there is any account of a southern Republican state convention better than those he wrote, it has not been taken from the book.

The dean of the corps of correspondents—and it was a large corps—was, of course, the venerable Edward Jones Hale, of New York. His long and successful life in newspaper work in the original *Observer* at Fayetteville intuitively gave him the talent for selecting topics that would be interesting, attractive, and elevating to his readers. Few could tell more directly or in more felicitous phrase exactly what he wanted to tell. His lines read like Goldsmith's. And Mr. Hale's New York letters were a prime feature in a Sunday paper.

For a long time it was a most perplexing question for the reading public as to who wrote the extraordinary articles called "Sunday Reading." One day they would make the Methodists wince, another the Baptists glad, another the Presbyterians grieve, and a fourth the Episcopalians murmur. But there was so much in any one of them that all could delight in that still they guessed and still the wonder grew that any Christian could write words so true. Perhaps not a baker's dozen in the capital knew or were quite sure that Governor Holden was their author. I fancy that there were hot-tempered people in those days (of course there are none now) who would have refused themselves the indulgence of reading these lay sermons if they had known who was in the pulpit; but even these worthy people, if they had known the genuine good it did his lonely heart to write them, would have read them in the spirit of penance for their thoughts.

* * * * * *

This picture of men and manners on the Raleigh *Observer* is painted with what may seem unnecessary detail.

But I am hopeful that there will be a few young spirits who will be glad of the truth; a few of our young journalists who will be proud to know that when they set their feet in the path of tolerance and fearlessness, they will find footprints already pressed into the soil.

In a day when poverty was too real and too familiar for men to underrate the power of money, the *Observer* lifted its journalistic standard far above the counting house. In the end, the counting house won its inevitable victory, but meanwhile, for a fine space, a free voice made itself heard through the state. Even today, the state is better therefor. The *Observer* is an untarnished tradition. It would be a pity if we forgot to remember it.

Chapter XVI

HENRY GRADY AND THE NEW SOUTH: EXPOSITIONS AND INDUSTRIAL DEVELOPMENT

THE prophet who foretold the great industrial development in the South was, in my judgment, Henry Grady, editor of the Atlanta *Constitution*, when he announced that a big cotton exposition of the South was needed and must be had.

There had been spread before the world at the Centennial in Philadelphia a wonderful picture of what the labor of the world was about. Gazing upon this picture, a million minds had been educated in the art of doing similar things. So Grady perceived what he could accomplish if in the same objective fashion he could show the southern people what a single plant could do for them. His aim was to educate first the people of the South and then the whole people of the country in the science of cotton. He wanted to show them that this single product, trebled in value since the Civil War, could—if intelligently used—rebuild much that had been lost and begin a new prosperity.

Nothing but genius could have drawn around him such a coterie of sympathetic apostles as Charles R. Miller of the New York *Times*, Walter Page of the Brooklyn *Eagle*, Moses P. Handy of the Philadelphia *Press*, and other lesser lights in the great business of making newspapers. He could understand that Cæsar himself could not have been Cæsar without Labienus,—in other words, that lieutenants were wanted to hold up his hand; and he chose his lieutenants with rare discrimination.

The Exposition at Atlanta was to be a kindergarten for people who had seen little and hence would remember much and who would spread by word of mouth what their eyes should see. His campaign was psychologically right and his industry in putting it into effect never failed. He was the first, so far as I know, to use a peripatetic stenographer and to weave into a first-hand story what each exhibitor had to say of his own exhibit and of the section which it represented. He talked with the exhibitors freely and would have his faithful scribe take down everything useful or quaint that was said, so that each day's *Constitution* had a fresh story. In this way there was spread in the press a series of pictures which otherwise would have been impossible. And they were seen by perceptive eyes, for such contributors as "Old Si" (Sam Small) and "Uncle Remus" (Joel Chandler Harris) made the *Constitution* a choice bit of literature not only for the common reader but for the "high brows."

In the Atlanta Exposition Henry Grady took time from the tangled mass of Georgia politics, which he dearly loved, to do something really great, not only for his city and state and section, but for the whole country. He quit making governors and senators to restore energy to communities and comfort to individual homes.

One product of the enthusiasm engendered was the *Industrial Review*. This was the first journal of its kind, so far as I know, of any national scope and was the forerunner of the *Manufacturers' Record* which has been and is today a marvel of excellence in its line. It was most gratifying to me to be invited to be one of the founders of and contributors to the *Industrial Review;* and through

it I gained stimulating association with such men as
Charles R. Miller, who became editor of the New York
Times and was for thirty years one of the really great
editors of the nineteenth century; Moses P. Handy, who
revived and established successfully the Philadelphia
Press and who later served as head of the publicity feature
of the Columbian Exposition; Balch, a brilliant reporter
and a genuine Sherlock Holmes. (He discovered and had
punished the murderer in one of the most shocking
crimes ever committed in a large eastern city.)

The Atlanta Exposition was the pioneer work in this
line for the South and for North Carolina, which to me
always stands for the South. Using much of the same
material, the state, in 1883, made an exhibit of great
merit at the Mechanics Institute Exposition held in
Boston.

Through correspondence between the Hon. Edward
Atkinson, a publicist-economist of distinction, and Dr.
Dabney, our state chemist, came the suggestion that
North Carolina should take a part in this Fair, and Governor Jarvis, Chairman of the Board of Agriculture, whose
province it was to care for the state's interests in this respect, at once became actively interested in it. The Board
directed that material be collected and shipped to Boston
to present a survey of the state's resources and to invite
the interest of those who might have in mind a change of
home.

Governor Jarvis seemed to fit into the joint of the times;
and he accomplished much during his administration in
putting the state in a favorable position abroad. He went
in person to Boston and led what it is not an extravagance
to call a crusade of good will into New England. The
ground had been broken through the Atkinson-Dabney

correspondence and the people of New England responded
to the sentiment which made the Exposition possible.
One can hardly exaggerate the courtesy of the officials,
the interested curiosity of visitors to the fair, and the
honestly offered and untiring hospitality and assistance
given to the officers of the exhibit by the Boston press.
The North Carolina Press Association was induced to
have its annual meeting in Boston instead of in a home
town, and at the meeting Governor Jarvis made a most
notable appearance. He was not as tall as one of the long
leaf pines in his native county of Currituck, but he was
as erect, and he stood above the heads of ordinary men.
He carried the good will and the hopes of his people into
New England, speaking without complaint and without
reproach of the past, with hope for the future, and by
the authority of his people.

He had such able and eloquent lieutenants as the Commissioner of Agriculture, Mr. McGehee, who recalled his
Harvard days; and a former Commissioner, Colonel Polk,
a soldier who could find comrades in courage here on the
other side of the battle field. The eloquence of these men
and the hospitable gatherings of the newspaper men held
the candle for the wonderful oration subsequently made
by Henry Grady before the New England Society, which
has become one of the classics in American oratory.

General Butler was then Governor of Massachusetts
and there was an interesting contrast between aristocratic Boston and the democratic state administration.
This was the very Ben Butler whose military rule over
conquered New Orleans had inspired such gorgeous Gallic
hatred. One recalls the story of the Creole who was reminded by an argumentative northerner that at least

they had no yellow fever in New Orleans during Ben Butler's régime.

"General Butlair and the yellow fevair the same year!" exclaimed the horrified Louisianian. "Impossible!"

By a rather singular coincidence our own Governor Jarvis had been forced into temporary residence at the Yarborough Hotel after the old mansion had become the Centennial Graded School and before the new mansion was completed; and we found the Governor of Massachusetts also domiciled in a hotel, the celebrated Revere House, where he was given to a most democratic hospitality. When he visited our exhibit, which he did through courtesy, he seemed much more interested in the motive behind the exposition than in what the state presented.

Among other visitors was the short, stubby Scotch scientist, Sir Lionel Playfair, a great chemist who seemed never to tire of looking at the variety of minerals and was especially pleased with specimens of leopardite from Mecklenburg. Professor Sargent, a great botanist, suggested the arrangement of the wonderful range of botanical products which the state displayed; and in company with Mr. Edward Kidder, catalogued them for us. Dr. Alexander Agassiz, a great son of a greater father, was so delighted with a slab of curly poplar in our exhibit that he took it to his private workshop and polished it for us, bringing into effect all its pictorial possibilities which his trained eye had perceived. George Abbot James, brother-in-law of Senator Lodge, introduced us to the clubs. Nothing in the way of social amenities was left undone. It was an experience which effectually taught us to separate the noun "hospitality" from the qualifying adjective "Southern."

10

The high average intelligence of the visitors kept all those who were connected with the state's exhibit at a high pitch of attention. And to show us that Massachusetts had progress for us to pattern after, the authorities had us visit the gigantic textile mills at Lowell and Nashua.

Mr. McGehee and I paid a visit to Governor Butler at his quarters in the Revere House, to thank him for the courtesies which he had personally and by proxy extended to our state. It was a most interesting evening. The Governor ordered his valet to bring out some particularly old and fragrant Medford rum which he had made into hot rum punches. Over these, he talked in entertaining fashion about his experiences in North Carolina where he had done some poor soldiering. His fund of anecdote was abundant and delightful and his cherished prejudices, while startling, were amusing. In the course of the conversation he took up the character of George Washington and of all the excoriations that I have ever heard, I think this was the greatest. He magnified the peccadilloes of the Father of his Country into high misdemeanors and seemed to take delight in detracting from him. The thing was so extravagant that one could but suspect him of amusing himself and shocking us to add to that amusement. At all events, the recent "publicity stunt" of an American novelist in scandalizing the nation by insisting that our first President was human, was in comparison with Ben Butler's diatribe a very mild performance.

Later I heard Governor Butler speak publicly in Faneuil Hall and I have never seen equaled the demonstration of popular favor which greeted him. People fought for places of vantage to see and hear him. He was the sort of man to inspire emotional intensity; whether people hated or admired him, they did it thoroughly.

The art of expositions was now beginning to be a habit. New Orleans, at the mouth of the greatest river valley in the world, could not consent to see Atlanta emphasize the possibilities of the plant with which the ships in her own port were loaded, and not intensify the emphasis by a bit of French accent. So a second cotton exposition was held at New Orleans. North Carolina, still utilizing as a nucleus the material gathered for the two previous expositions, was one of the foremost states represented in this fair, the success of which was second only to the Centennial at Philadelphia.

The New Orleans Exposition was national in its scope. All the northern states in a peaceful invasion established themselves in the bosom of the South and it would be difficult to overestimate the effect of the association in bringing about a cordial state of feeling between the North and the South, or the educational good accomplished by bringing many thousands of people from all sections to see with their own eyes the problems with which the people of the South had to contend and the means by which they purposed to work out a desirable future.

Colonel E. A. Burke was the manager of this Exposition. He engaged Dr. Dabney, head of the North Carolina Experiment Station, and myself on account of our previous experience in such work to take part in its construction and development. This gave us the opportunity of being familiar with every feature of it, more or less; and—in a fair way—to get advantageous position for our own state.

The hospitality of New Orleans was of that peculiar flavor which a seasoning of Latin courtesy can give. Delightful.

Governor Scales joined the two state commissioners, the distinguished Judge Howard and Major Morehead (who did so much in later years to make useful acetylene gas and aluminum) in a visit to the Exposition and an inspection of North Carolina's exhibit. He was greatly pleased and afterwards when the extravagance of the State Department of Agriculture, in making the exhibit, was attacked for reasons that hardly rose to the ordinary political level, the Governor was able to tell first hand what he had seen,—what the state had tried to do and what it had done at New Orleans. The result of this investigation was quite amusing. The investigating committee found that there had been an extravagant expenditure of $3.90, which had been applied in the way of tips to the lordly porters of sleeping cars *et al.;* and with this laboring of the mountain, the criticism ran after the mouse!

Among the most useful men connected with the New Orleans Exposition was Joseph A. Holmes, the then professor of Botany at the University. The industrious attention which he gave to any matter entrusted to him foreshadowed his usefulness to the state in every department in which he served; and his wider usefulness to the nation and to humanity in his final work as creator and director of our national Bureau of Mines. When he literally laid down his life for his fellows, he was appropriately followed to his last resting place by such intimate friends as General Gorgas and Governor Pinchot, men whose scientific and patriotic attainments rank them not only as great Americans, but as benefactors of mankind. Joseph Holmes was of their company.

His brother Nicholas J. Holmes had been an old schoolmate of mine at Edinburgh. And I found it true of both of them that they were occupied only with essentials. They never wasted life by magnifying material values.

When Joseph Holmes was traveling in Belgium, some years before he attained to high official position, he remarked to the proprietor of the hotel where he was stopping that he would very much like to talk with the King (the great old Leopold was then reigning) about mining matters. The innkeeper was appalled. Talk to the King! These Americans! But Dr. Holmes kept repeating his wish to one person and another and eventually it was carried to the King's ears. With the keenness that made him a great ruler, Leopold recognized that it was to his interest to talk with a man who could teach him much. An audience was arranged. Dr. Holmes, who was traveling simply, had no dress suit. An ordinary man, magnifying small matters, would have been upset by this circumstance. Not Dr. Holmes. He attended the audience in his sack coat. There was another audience and another. For the King who had seen millions of dress suits had not seen another man who knew the subject of conserving human life in the depths of the earth as Dr. Holmes knew that subject. Joseph Holmes was one of the few persons I have ever known who were entirely without vanity.

His genuine modesty kept Dr. Holmes from writing his name across the movements which he initiated or furthered; the state owes him many an unrecognized debt today. For instance, how many people remember the pioneer work which he and Sydenham Alexander did for good roads? The limousines which travel our smooth highways today could not roll so proudly if Dr. Holmes had not preceded them in his old demonstration buggy from which he preached to the country people the necessity for easy communication and transportation.

Nicholas J. Holmes, his brother, was concerned with saving life too, saving it for eternity. Early in his career, he abandoned the law and turned to the prophets. He became a minister of the Gospel and drew about him a group who shared his simple, profound faith. They lived on a mountain in South Carolina. Both literally and figuratively they lived on a mountain. Taking no thought for the morrow, they followed Christ without reservation. When his brother Joseph died, Nicholas came to Washington and stayed for a few days in my household. I can hardly describe the effect of that brief visit. The whole household felt it. Although he was taciturn and talked not at all of his religion unless directly questioned, yet his presence was an exquisite benediction upon the house. His personality was stripped to spiritual essentials.

Truly unworldly men like these two Holmes brothers prove the Christian dogmas far more effectually than argumentative theologians. It is good to have known them. And even back in the New Orleans days those of us who were associated with Joseph Holmes were dimly conscious of the quality of the man.

In briefly sketching the New Orleans fair, I would not like to omit the services of Blanche K. Bruce, one time United States Senator from the State of Mississippi, and at this Exposition in charge of the exhibits made by the colored people. He was indefatigable in his work and took a becoming pride in seeing that his people got what was their due, as well as that they should make creditable illustration of the work that they had done since they had embarked upon freedom. He was most courteous in his manner, punctual in his duties; a fine statesman of his race.

In preparing our state's exhibit at New Orleans, we got together many beautiful specimens of native woods. Riding through the mountain trails called roads, hunting specimens of timber and minerals which should prove to a nation our potential wealth, was wholesome work. It brought one into contact with men who knew these things first-hand and who would guide and interest. It was not all work. There was recreation in it.

For instance, to visit the six-thousand foot top of Roan Mountain, the loftiest meadow east of the Rockies, covered with heavy green grass, fringed with small stunted pines—above the timber line. On a cliff on the edge of this plateau was a log hotel with broad fireplaces and broad porches. The hotel was owned by General Wilder, an officer of distinction in the Civil War, who had fought in the battle above the clouds—Missionary Ridge—and who had cut no mean figure there. To hear him talk of his experiences was a night well spent. And there was, too, a guest from New Orleans, Mrs. Ruth McEnery Stuart, who wrote unequaled stories in dialect, stories of subduing pathos. She had an only son, an intensely beautiful boy. To be allowed to sit in her company and hear her tell the lad the folk tales of her old home was an experience to be cherished all one's days. She made us feel that we were welcome to share her stories with the boy, that beautiful boy,—it was worth a climb up six thousand feet to see him.

Once again, in preparing the state's exhibit for the Columbian Fair at Chicago, we had to scramble up and slide down the mountainsides, gathering timber. I recall an evening when we rested on the porch of his house with one John Randolph, a man of importance in his community, and listened to the Toe River go by in the August moonlight. After talking over the programme for the next day and getting the routes mapped out, our conversation turned to fishing. We gave some account of the fishing in Eastern Carolina waters where trolling would bring in a multitude of Spanish mackerel and it was a man's job to land a superb blue fish. A young lad who had been very attentive to the talk asked eagerly what we meant when we spoke of the "tide" which ebbed and flowed. When a few words had made clear the idea of the water's periodic rise and fall, he followed his question with a more difficult one. "What makes it do that?" he asked. With some hesitation, the accepted opinion was ventured that it was the effect of the moon on the water. The young man looked straight at the one who offered this explanation and said with perfect gravity—

"That's the durndest lie I ever heerd in my life and now I don't believe those other stories you been telling."

Well, it takes faith to scale mountains; science stumbles and falls.

We were much aided in collecting specimens of timber for the Chicago Fair by the generous gift of a North Carolinian whose citizenship was voluntary and not the accident of birth,—George W. Vanderbilt.

It would be a mistake to consider Mr. Vanderbilt simply as a very rich man. His riches had come to him in a way that he could not even have avoided. But he used his money to work out big problems and he grew more and more, as his years increased, to the stature of a master builder.

He was the youngest son of Cornelius Vanderbilt—the great old "commodore"; and he came to North Carolina with his mother in search of health. Her influence seems to have nurtured his governing idea which was home-building. He built a home on the dome of a great mountain among greater mountains, which was beautiful enough to be thus set upon the heights. His prolonged visit to Asheville naturally aroused curiosity as to whether he would make the town his residence. He had the good fortune to have a great doctor as his adviser and his friend. To Dr. Westray Battle he outlined his plans and spoke modestly of what he thought he could do for his generation in building a home which would be like a light set upon a hill for those who would care to be guided by this light.

In conversation with Dr. Battle, I asked him if he thought Mr. Vanderbilt would make his home in the North Carolina mountains. His answer was, "Consult the augurs. If he lives well through the cherry season, he will live here always." Dr. Battle then explained that the cherry season meant that season when there is more sickness in the mountain country than in any other, and if the distinguished visitor escaped this depressing influence, then his growing love for the country would doubtless persuade him to adopt it as his home.

What he did the world knows. Around his model home he built a model town. With his scientific dairy where, to our provincial eyes, the cows seemed to be positively coddled, he showed a community how to produce germless milk. And with the perfect little hospital which he established he returned to thousands of sufferers that gift of health which he had himself received on the life-giving mountain tops. Mr. Vanderbilt never built factories, never developed power, never took interest in what may be called commercial ventures; but turned his great income and capital into the improvement of that fundamental institution, the home. While Biltmore can be seen, the lesson which the founder of Biltmore sought to teach will still be read. He was a North Carolinian by choice and he gave us cause to be honestly proud of that choice.

As his mother inaugurated his interest in the state, so his wife carried on his fine work after he died. Her interest in agricultural education and her notable work along this line was recognized in her election as first woman president of our State Fair.

It was George Vanderbilt who brought Gifford Pinchot to North Carolina as forester for the Biltmore estate, and Mr. Vanderbilt's gift to the state exhibit at Chicago was used under Mr. Pinchot's direction to make a display of woods and timbers. This early work, successfully accomplished, was the preliminary of Mr. Pinchot's later work as Chief of the Forestry Bureau of the United States, where he became the powerful prophet of conservation.

The World's Fair at Chicago was the climax of the great international fairs. It went far beyond its predecessors and for another half century it can only have imitations. Current history said of it that it was the only enterprise of importance which did not feel the depression of the panic and the suspension of trade; its success was brilliant and unbroken. George Ade, in a recent magazine article, has thus valued it:

The world's greatest achievement for the departing century was pulled off in Chicago. The Columbian Exposition was the most stupendous, interesting and significant show ever spread out for the public. As a demonstration of civic pride, community enterprise and nation-wide cooperation, it has not been matched during the thirty-three years which have slid rapidly away since it bloomed in splendor on the shores of Lake Michigan. That city of gigantic white buildings, fluttering a myriad of flags, and revealing the progress and culture and creative impulses of the whole world, made the Centennial and the Interstate Exposition look like side-shows.

It tacked holiday bunting on a woeful period of business depression which was slowly hatching out Free Silver and William Jennings Bryan.

As executive commissioner for our state, I came naturally into close touch with all of our representatives in Chicago and I know that they *were* finely representative.

Under the Federal Act providing for the Exposition, Col. A. B. Andrews, Vice President of the Southern Railway and a recognized leader in the railroad world, and Colonel Thomas B. Keogh, Secretary of the National Republican Committee, were named commissioners. Mrs. George W. Kidder and Mrs. Charles Price were commissioners for the Woman's Department. Governor Carr had also appointed Mrs. Robert R. Cotten as alternate commissioner. This was the first commission to an international exposition where the state had made equality in representation and where women came into their own.

In charge of the Department of Forestry was Gifford Pinchot; and of Fisheries, Herbert Brimley. T. K. Bruner, Secretary of the Board, was distinguished for his skill and taste in devising attractive installation of our exhibits.

The women commissioners were successful in bringing together everything that illustrated the work of home making, from the decorative antiques of colonial days to the homely products of the farms of the nineties. Mrs. Kidder was one of the founders of the national society of Colonial Dames and later became a high official in that patriotic organization. Mrs. Price gave intelligence and assiduity to the duties of her position. Mrs. Peter Wilson was chosen a judge of the foreign and domestic cotton exhibits and wrote the report on these exhibits which was approved and accepted.

Mrs. Cotten began at Chicago her public work which has carried her in later years to the forefront of national organizations working for the betterment of living conditions for women and children. She has been a pioneer of the finest sort of feminism in North Carolina and the women of the state owe her a very real debt. All of us— men and women—owe her a further debt for her patriotism in preserving our earliest history in her interesting poem, "The White Doe." The legend of North Carolina's first woman-child is delightfully told in this poetic narrative written by the woman who has done so much to improve conditions of life for all women and children in the state.

Mrs. Cotten completed her artistic contribution to local history in a most interesting way when she procured for the state a truly beautiful statue of Virginia Dare. Miss Lander, a New England sculptress of distinction who had fashioned the image, was already an old lady when her friendship with Mrs. Cotten began. She lived in Washington City in a roomy, comfortable home filled with things of beauty. Her memory too was stored with interesting and beautiful things, not least of which was her friendship with Hawthorne. But in her closing years, her affection seemed to center upon the lovely marble maiden she had created,—her statue of Virginia Dare. She had placed it in a bay window where the eastern sun bathed it in the mornings; and sometimes coming into the room she would exclaim, "Virginia, my dear, you are beautiful today!" Virginia was her creation and had become to her almost like a human child. Naturally she could not make up her mind to part with the statue while she lived. But she was persuaded by Mrs. Cotten that the proper resting place for Virginia Dare would be the state of her birth; and so, in her will, she left the statue to North Carolina. Her recent death has brought this genuine treasure into the possession of our state.

Chapter XVII

COLONEL POLK AND THE FARMERS: JOHN T. PATRICK AND ADVERTISING

WHILE serving as Secretary of the State Board of Agriculture and as Commissioner of Immigration, I came in contact with two men who conformed to no pattern save of their own cutting but who, in strikingly individual ways, worked for the corporate good. Both of these men deserve from us the tribute of memory. One of them, L. L. Polk, although a state official, was really the spokesman for a class; for a class which at that time needed an advocate and which Page described in his imperishable phrase, "the forgotten man." The other—John T. Patrick —himself one of those very forgotten men, thought and worked always for the whole state.

Dr. Battle, the then President of the University, who was not particularly enamored of Colonel Polk, yet said of him that he possessed a style of speaking very acceptable to the people; and Mr. Ashe, the state historian, gives it as his opinion that Colonel Polk was admirably fitted for the work that he did. He was more than this, I take the opportunity of saying from long association with him.

He came out of the war with little more than his side arms and took his place in the ranks of the builders. By nature, he was a stirrer-up of friendly strife. There was nothing vicious about him, but he was entirely upon his side of the fence and was honestly convinced that all others were trespassers. So, in the ten years succeeding

flagrant and honorable warfare, when he saw or thought
he saw that the land owner and tiller had an inferior position in the economic scheme, his indignation magnified
the injustice. As a natural sequence of his resentful
thought along this line, he set out to acquaint the ag-
grieved with their grievances. His handsome figure and
sympathetic voice made him at once a favorite at public
gatherings. He delighted in crowds and they delighted in
him.

A singular aspect of his oratorical power recalls itself
to me. At Mount Holly, on the banks of the Catawba,
there gathered a large crowd of farmers. It was a sort of
harvest feast. A great circus tent hardly contained the
audience which Colonel Polk addressed and which he
swayed in a sort of delirium of satisfaction. He had invited me, although he knew that I was not in sympathy
with his plans or theories, to sit on the platform with him,
and placed thus within a few feet of him I noticed that
when he began to speak his knees trembled violently. In
the afternoon when we were resting in the hotel before
leaving the town, I spoke to him about this. He told me
that he never stood before an audience that this violent
muscular tremor did not pass over him; that his mouth
was as hot as a furnace and his pulse galloping; yet his
audience was looking upon a man with a smile upon his
face and apparently a placid delight in the opportunity
of talking with them.

Governor Vance liked him, saw his usefulness to himself and to the state, and made him one of his "pets"—
the name given to those who were in the governor's inner
circle by those who were on the outside. The governor
informed the Board of Agriculture of his wish that Colonel

Polk be commissioner and—by singular chance—the
Board found itself quite in agreement with his wish.

Colonel Polk made a very good commissioner, but he
soon grew restless in office, having no stomach for routine,
and resigned to become editorial traveling correspondent
of the principal paper in the state. Passing over some
lesser employments in business in which he had the rewards which come to unstable men, he encouraged the
organization of farmer societies,—the Grange, the Al-
liance, and lesser bodies; and in order to aid them more
effectively, he established a paper called *The Progressive
Farmer*. It has always been more or less successful. It
has run a fine course and has never veered from its main
purpose, though it has boxed the political compass and
has irritated many campaign managers. Today, under
wise and scholarly direction, it is one of the ablest papers
of its influential class. If he had done nothing but found
The Progressive Farmer, Colonel Polk should have a name
in the state.

He became a popular leader in the great agrarian
movement which culminated in bringing together all agricultural associations into the People's or Populist Party.
He practically wrote the Ocala Platform, a name not much
used now but which at that time represented a hodge-
podge of all the wild theories advanced for government.
(It is not amiss to say that within a generation every
plank of it has been built into the platforms of the two
major parties and, with the exception of the theory of
silver, sixteen-to-one, most of its principles have been
translated into legal statutes. Another amusing illustration of the familiar paradox that today's heterodoxy is
tomorrow's orthodoxy.)

Colonel Polk could have had the nomination for the presidency when Weaver was chosen by the Populists for the funeral pyre. I have seen correspondence which I think does not leave this in doubt. The Goddess of Wisdom was for once kind to him, however, and he shoved the nomination aside. He was then on the crest of his highest wave, banqueted when he returned to his native state and heartily cheered when he went into any assembly of his people.

There was never any rest for his restlessness until he accepted the enforced peace of death. He passed away in Washington city, with his family gathered about him, at Providence Hospital, where he was ministered unto by the kindly Catholic sisters, whose quiet abnegation of life must have seemed strange to his crusading spirit.

A second Carolina crusader was John T. Patrick, who gave forty years of his life in making North Carolina find herself in the great growth in which she now leads among southern states. His plan was as simple as General Forrest's explanation of the art of war. He was an advertiser by nature and self-culture.

He came unsolicited before the Board of Agriculture and Immigration with a plan to interest northern men and money in the state. His figure and fashion announced him from the village; his luminous eyes were at once confident and confiding. His proposition was very simple, very crude, but it worked. It planned to exchange land in North Carolina for space in northern newspapers. The Board was to give him a living salary for one year and recognize his plan. In return he gave twelve hundred acres of land, embracing the highest point in the long leaf pine region, the summit of a sea of pines, on an important railway, free from debt, with a good title. The

11

land was then worth say $1,200; now many thousands of
dollars. This land was to be subdivided into lots which
were to be given in exchange for space in northern weekly
newspapers carrying an advertisement of the whole state's
resources and opportunities and emphasizing the restora-
tion to health to be had in the balsam-laden atmosphere
of this pine region. He got the papers to accept the plan
and in this way sold the town of Southern Pines to them.
The papers resold the lots to purchasers at a greater or
less profit and the movement was established for the making of Southern Pines, now a great winter resort.

Patrick, the first great private promoter of North Carolina, was in himself proof that a crop was coming up in
the field which the state had plowed. The state, through
its expositions, had brought about two results; it had
educated our own people as to what they had done and
could do, and it had insured a quicker development by
offering to others a share in what we had. The old in-
junction "Know this," and the historic cry, "come over
into Macedonia and help us," had been combined in the
state's official advertising campaign.

A sort of season had been brought about favorable to
growth. It would be beyond the truth to suggest more
than this because individual foresight and initiative and
courage were the determining factors. The state had
grown the bean stalk and now Jack was about to climb
up until he was literally among the giants.

At first he climbed too fast. Buoyant enthusiasm
brought about a reckless speculation in real estate which
left individual losses that it would take a census gatherer
to enumerate but which left also a spirit of ambition great
enough to achieve such cities as the Winston-Salem that
we know today. I take a satisfying pride in the prophetic

part which I myself took in the promotion of our hyphen-
ated metropolis. I believed then, as I know now, that it
was impossible to exaggerate the outcome of the spirit of
the community in combination with the ideal physical
conditions surrounding the town.

The momentum of industrial development was too
great to be checked by temporary setbacks; and it was
so great that it set in motion another development which
is familiarly known as the educational movement.

The leaders of the educational movement from the very
beginning of their efforts stood out from among the
people, tall and straight. The generals of the industrial
development, on the other hand, did not emerge into publicity until they had brought their campaigns to spectacular victory. Hence, although the effort for intellectual progress was a logical outgrowth of the expanding
industrial activity, yet the leaders of the second movement precede the leaders of the first movement on the
historical screen.

Chapter XVIII

EDUCATIONAL MOVEMENT IN NORTH CARO-
LINA: THE WATAUGANS AND A
FEW FREE LANCES

IF one were a philosopher, he might trace the movement for more and better education in the state to some interestingly obscure source and give good reasons for his reasoning. But to a wayfaring man who has been hurried through the years by pressure of changes, the Watauga Club stands out as a sort of guide post.

This club was daring enough to think that the then governing element had served its greatest usefulness and might be replaced by something equally as good. Such a supposition was, of course, profane, because it laid a questioning hand on the past. However, certain fellows of a youngish but thoughtful sort, unafraid of epithets, banded themselves together not to tear down but to break camp and go forward.

Such men as Alderman, Daniels, Dabney, Joyner, McIver, Page, Peele, and a line full of others were born to love of home and were, therefore, patriots. They had a few unwise associates who wanted to pull down the University and this set against the club the intelligent prejudice of the state, but the impediment to the good work of the Watauga organization thus manufactured did not in the end prove serious.

The object of the club was first of all to organize an effort to teach agriculture and then its adjunct, mechanics. Very practical as a program, nothing to cause unrest. But the unrest was already there. One reads that there was unrest before ever Peter the Hermit preached the crusades, but he gave direction to the agitation and pointed out the distinct goal. That is pretty much what our educational prophets did for us.

McIver was the queen bee in the hive.

Living in the very center of the state, Charles D. McIver got hold of a nugget of golden truth that any one of us might have stumbled upon. That was the belief and theory that if one could educate the mothers of the state, there would be no more ignorant children. Doubtless others had said the same thing; God knows they had thought it;—but McIver pictured it like a rainbow in the sky. His hearers took up his words and repeated them to all whom they met.

A people who had made race, sex, and age prerequisite to suffrage were not unused to the idea of subjection. They had to be wrenched from their stanchions. McIver was the ideal man to do this wrenching. He approached the people from the angle of an understanding heart. They could be persuaded by him because they could understand him.

It would perhaps be unfair to the lower public opinion to say that it was opposed to education. It was not conscious of its ignorance. But many of us dear old Bourbons thought it would be dangerous to thrust general education too suddenly upon the mass of the people. Such cautious fears did not deter this Calvinist who would go to any length for his belief. He was not an orator, and was not an actor, not a mouther of words, but a doer of things. And perhaps his greatest strength lay in the fact that he was an interpreter who could translate the desire of a class into the purpose of the mass.

It was once my agreeable privilege to introduce Mr. McIver to the venerable and wise Senator Hoar of Massachusetts as a man who had educated five thousand women. There was a genuine humility in the voice and manner of the New England statesman as he said:

"I bow to a man who has educated five thousand of the mothers that are to be."

After shaking hands they walked away together, I remember. They understood each other. As the Massachusetts man spoke then, North Carolina feels today.

Edwin A. Alderman. There was an unconscious and unintentional aloofness about Alderman that did not attach to his co-workers. They were all gentlemen, but he was a gentleman to the tips of his fingers. His standards were higher than the standards of ordinary men and he lived up to them with the most extraordinary consistency. It was this real superiority which set him apart from his fellows, and not any sense of superiority.

From his youth up, in the most graceful manner, he had equal manly sympathy for the weak and the strong; he was born to beautiful service. He was a natural teacher and the obligation which he put upon himself of showing others what he knew made him an orator.

The first time that I saw him was when he was professor of history in the North Carolina College for Women of which McIver was president. He seemed then in danger of being a man addicted to vice-presidencies, but that was because there had been no opportunity to show his capacity for development in higher lines. With McIver he was carrying a love for education about the state, offering it in high and low places. But where McIver always said, "We will," Alderman would say, "You should." That seems to me the difference between these two really great men; one was a preacher and the other a teacher.

Soon he was called to the presidency of the University, where he was bred. After an honorable administration there, he went to Tulane University and in that elegant, grateful, and Gallic atmosphere he beautified his talents.

Finally he was called upon to guard the twin product of Jefferson's genius at the foot of Ragged Mountain. I say *twin* product, because the University of Virginia is more than a seat of learning; it is a depository of Jeffersonian faith. We have wandered from that faith of late years. Even the Democratic party, which had its birth at Monticello, has been following after strange gods. But here and there a voice is raised to call us out of this wilderness of intolerance and lawlessness, with its undergrowth of dead materialism, into the old freedom and spaciousness of Jefferson's truth. The most compelling of these voices should come from the mountain out of which proceeded the spirit of our faith. And from that mountain we can hear it now, clear and challenging. Alderman has been the soul of renaissance of the original spirit of the University of Virginia.

Alderman does not belong to the rhetorical school of orators. He does not pour old platitudes into ornamental phrases. But he knows how to match a word to a thought. I once said to a great Virginia orator, the last of the old school, that I had heard that Alderman had made a wonderful speech before the Virginia legislature. Perhaps he thought "wonderful" an indiscreet adjective. He said, with a coolness in his voice that could be felt some distance, "I understand he speaks very well." I determined then that I would hear him speak for myself. And eventually I did. Before an audience that comprised the highest officials of our country and the diplomatic representatives of all the nations of the earth, I heard him tell the story of Woodrow Wilson. I had heard Wilson himself from the same dais, and I am quite sure that Alderman spoke better than Wilson. In Washington, a city grown almost deaf to oratory, the perfection of his simple periods made a genuine sensation. But before the acclaim which followed in the wake of his retirement from the rostrum had spent itself, he slipped away from the crowd, accompanied by a close personal friend, and together they sought out an old associate of former years. This was very human and I mention it here because it broadens the skyline of his high life.

Further illustration of his intrinsic fineness is not needed, but it is delightful to add that when the board of trustees of the University, appreciating the value of his services, proposed a very large addition to his salary, he promptly declined it unless they could see their way proportionately to increase the salaries of his co-workers. That was good fellowship, unselfish fellowship.

A man of his talents has naturally not lacked opportunity to make his own fortune. There was a time, I remember, when he was offered the presidency of a great insurance company, a position with highly tempting financial possibilities. But having spent his strength for so many years in insuring young men against life and not against death, he thought it better to continue signing diplomas, rather than policies.

Talking of Alderman makes one feel like talking gossip. There are so many pleasant things one would like to say about him.

Josephus Daniels was one of the foremost members of the Watauga Club. He has never had the credit for his part of the work which the club did. He comprehended the scheme of its outlook and sympathized thoroughly with it; and in addition he had a practical knowledge of what the movement was up against. He knew how slowly a revolutionary project moves when it touches the pocket-book. Perhaps the average citizen was not at heart in favor of the ignorance of the masses, but still he weighed it in the balance with high taxes. Having grown up in a community with well-to-do ignorance, Josephus Daniels knew that it was no easy matter to teach people to enlarge their views.

He was the treasurer of the movement, not as the keeper of its moneys, because there were no moneys. A scrip and a staff constituted the outfit of the Wataugans. But he had a newspaper in which were deposited the thoughts, plans, and hopes of this band of conspirators against the complacent peacefulness of the state's policies. Out of it was distributed the literature of the movement. It would not do to say that the general press of the state was hostile to the admitted need of the children of the state, nor that it tried to suppress this effort to better conditions. It just did not *see* the situation and busied itself with a more common bread and meat business as one day followed another.

A second reason which nudges me to the belief that Daniels has not had his full wages for work done is the consideration that he was not an orator in the sense that Alderman was. Neither did he have the superior platform presence and challenging wit that Page had. Yet he spoke well, even though he was a novice at it. And he has spoken better and better until today there is always an audience for him whenever and wherever he wishes to speak.

He has gone forward all the time and has grown steadily. This capacity for continued growth is, I think, his most unusual quality; because nearly all men allow their minds and their characters to crystallize after they have moulded their lives into some fullness of success.

Today Josephus Daniels is the most outstanding and withstanding member of the celebrated Wilson cabinet. One can berate him for all sorts of mistakes, and persons with limited mental equipment can laugh at his indifference to those meticulous details of official etiquette which have nothing to do with real gentility,—but out of it, through divine providence and a diviner genius for labor, he has come to fill a niche in our national history and to fill it admirably.

There is always a sort of impertinence in analyzing the motives and the purposes of a man. Even a man in the limelight of public life is entitled to the privacy of his own mind and soul. But I am going to risk this impertinence in order to define what has seemed to me Josephus Daniels's greatest, but his least-known, victory.

By his own genuine friendliness and his very charming hospitality—I wonder if North Carolinians appreciate the reputation that he won in Washington as a host?—Josephus Daniels has made a multitude of personal friends. But he has also made many public enemies by an insistent non-conformity and by a tendency to magnify the wickedness of offenses which the world considers venial. It was these traits which made his career in our own state so stormy; and when he came to Washington as Secretary of the Navy, the same traits brought upon him a veritable barrage of ridicule. The hardest thing in the world to stand up against is ridicule and to his credit be it said that Mr. Daniels stood unflinchingly. It was moral cour-

age worthy of a broader cause. But that is not the biggest
thing he did.

Our country went into the World War. And with the
declaration of war, Josephus Daniels instantly put aside
his personal warfare against the cliques in the navy which
were hostile to him. From that moment he thought of the
one vital necessity—to win. He chose men for places
where fitness meant life or death for thousands. And he
chose the fittest men. It mattered not now whether those
men had stood for or against his own policies. I have it
on the word of a member of the General Board which
directed the naval operations during the war period that
Mr. Daniels subordinated every personal prejudice to the
general executive good.

The result is history. There is not an administration of
our navy which can match his achievement in carrying
an army of two million men to a foreign shore and bringing them home again without a loss of life. Future generations will know his part in the victory of 1918. But we,
his contemporaries, ought to know of that great and
precedent victory, his victory over himself. A man past
middle-age, standing at the center of a maelstrom of war,
taught himself—for nobody else taught him—to recognize the difference between essentials and non-essentials,
and to choose the essential. His choice helped to win for
us the war. If his commander-in-chief had won such a
victory over *himself*, *he* might have won the peace.

Walter Hines Page! The very name is exclamatory.

But it is not of the ambassador to the greatest power
on earth, the familiar of kings and the intercessor in time
of supreme stress for even hostile peoples, that I would
speak. Nor is it of the maker of great newspapers, nor of

the author of a book that worked a frenzy amongst a multitude of readers, nor of the writer who fashioned the great prose poem, "The Forgotten Man." No; I would recall Walt Page, the editor of a town paper, a town called "city" by virtue of its being a capital; Walt Page, member of and almost chief offender in that Guy Fawkes organization, the Watauga Club.

He had so many and such inconsistent excellencies that they refuse to be catalogued. There was an earnestness about him, and a quizzical seriousness that impressed and sometimes offended those with whom he came in contact. He was a great force and did much in the years before he left home to put his name at the head of the roster of great North Carolinians.

Like all the Pages, he was born and bred beneath the stately pines under whose thin shadows they played and worked. He and they were like these pines, straight and with their beauty in their crests. They made a tribe almost in themselves in the sandhills.

He was no orator in the sense of weaving fine periods but he had a humorous, ironical capacity for stating facts which was abashing to those in contest with him. Having once seen him in action, one could not forget him.

His irrepressible humor broke out on the most august occasions. In the more spacious years of his later life, it did not even spare the shovel hat and knee breeches of a British Lord Spiritual. When the Archbishop of Canterbury rather casually invited him to dinner, meeting him one day in the street, and he hesitated for a moment, the Bishop assured him that the affair was not to be very formal,—"only a few bishops and yourself." Without a smile, Page replied that the bishops would be good enough

for him. "Good enough for you!" remonstrated the scan-
dalized prelate, as he stood aghast at such ecclesiastic
democracy. Eventually, however, he enjoyed it, especially after Page's clever daughter had given him a key
to the comedy.

The possessor of a strong sense of humor is apt to
possess also what some one has called "over minds,"—
detached faculties which stand apart, as it were, and watch
the very action in which their owner is taking part. Such
detachment often gives an impression of lack of sympathy.
It is hard for us to realize that a man may criticize us
without animus. Something of this sort I believe to have
been the explanation of the well-defined resentment
which grew up in North Carolina against Page and of a
similar resentment which one sometimes hears expressed
in other sections. The North Carolina resentment crystal-
lized after the publication of his novel; the feeling in
other parts of the country proceeded from the publication of his life and letters. North Carolinians assumed
that because he saw and described the South with detachment, he was hostile. And similarly certain excessively
patriotic Americans assumed that because he analyzed
American policies with a like detachment, he must be
anti-American and pro-British. Of course the opposite
was true. Walter Page criticized us because he loved us
and, therefore, desired for us perfection.

We are given to using the word "great" rather freely
in North Carolina. But we can use it without misgiving
when we apply it to Walter Page. We do not have to
explain it, even. That tablet in Westminster Abbey is
explanation enough. How proud we ought to be that a
branch of our long leaf pine has been twined through the
laurel which crowns the English tradition.

In Virginia, as in Scotland, there are two families of Dabneys,—the black Dabneys and the red Dabneys. Dr. Charles W. Dabney belonged essentially to the black Dabneys. Brought up in a Presbyterian college by his father, who was chief of staff to Stonewall Jackson, he galloped through American universities and came to North Carolina as a Ph.D. from Heidelberg to teach chemistry and to be the chief of the Agricultural Experiment Station. This opened up a field that he looked for and it was not long before he had discovered phosphates in the east and tin in the west and had set people to work in their development.

He was the scientific member of the Watauga Club and his name is familiar in the history of national expositions. He developed and enlarged the scientific branches of the United States Department of Agriculture, of which he became Assistant Secretary. Then returning to his earlier tastes, he became the president of two universities, in both of which he did notable work. These performances would seem to qualify him as a member of the Watauga Club. At the risk of repetition, the object of this club—awkwardly stated—was to carry education to the average man according to his wants. In agriculture first, because there were few who were not farmers; then, in the handicrafts. Dr. Dabney's highly trained technical understanding specially fitted him for this double service.

Of course, the attitude of the people toward the Watauga Club has changed. Success always turns a public menace into a public benefit and so we all believe in the Wataugans now. However, if we do not become obnoxiously boastful over these beginnings, there is much for us in the future.

A club that finally produced an ambassador, a Secretary of the Navy, an Assistant Secretary of Agriculture, a president of three universities, a president of two universities, the president of the State College for Women, and a state superintendent of public instruction, was not a measly affair. It awaits a counterpart.

Aycock's name is great enough to be written without any title. I confess that somehow I lacked that enthusiasm for his oratory which my friends entertained and constantly expressed. It was noised about that he was a new orator in a high sense, in a new cause. I never really heard him speak but once. A large audience had gathered at night in the courthouse at Asheville. The train on which he was to reach the city had been wrecked and the audience was wearied with waiting. The anxious moments were relieved by the bubbling cleverness, wit, and wisdom of Frank Winston. A shout went up the steps. Aycock was on the platform and without apology was in the full swing of a political speech. In a moment I had forgot my misgivings and I was swung along by his periods and his action just as those were who sat about me.

He did not have the dramatic part of the educational movement, but he did what was perhaps of as much importance. He popularized and solidified the sentiment of the state in the true doctrine which McIver, Alderman, and Daniels had carried to every hamlet; and as the governor of the state he spoke with authority. The most difficult of all tasks is to persuade others that they must deny themselves those things to which they attach great importance. Governor Aycock really proved to those who had property that it was their duty to give of it and to build up a condition which would make illiteracy impossible. The good that he did lives after him in the generous spirit in which all the schools of the state, from the village common school to the University, are supported by taxpayers great and small.

Joe Caldwell was not a Wataugan but as a free lance he worked to the same end.

He was a born editor. His instinct told him what North Carolina ought to think on any question of real interest and he proceeded in language that was as essentially his own as if it had been a patois to tell his readers that they *did* think it.

In a small way in connection with his paper, or as a part of it, he had what may be called, in a language that made no part of his vocabulary a "salon." That is to say, he had a knack of picking out rare spirits and welding them into his circle. There was John Charles McNeil, the poet of the pines, who delighted with his fancies; Isaac Avery, a writer of dashing short stories; Buck Bryant, whose tales of the chase could almost start the welkin ringing with the note of his horn; Howard Banks of clerical cut and clerical conduct, who wrote excellent stuff and still writes it; Abernethy, afterwards the head of the paper; and other lesser lights, but nevertheless, lights. Bryant and Banks never grow old and on big metropolitan dailies are reaping the rewards of their training with this editor born. The only instruction Joe Caldwell ever gave any man whom he sent out to get a story for his paper was, "Tell the truth. The truth only survives." He was so rarely given to preaching that doubtless this preachment surprised him.

The classic motto for perfect human development is so familiar to us that it is trite,—*Mens sana in corpore sano.* Perhaps it was its familiarity that made us forget it. Even the Wataugans, in their enthusiasm for the *mens sana* forgot the *corpus sanus*. But one among us remembered. Richard Lewis *knew* the inestimable value of health. And slowly he educated his state to know it. Without the gift of public health which we received at his gentle hands, neither our intellectual nor our industrial progress could have been measured by the encouraging results which we count so pridefully today.

Dick Lewis was too close to me for me to *see* him; I have always been able to put out my hand and feel him. But Judge Hoke estimated his value to the state with judicial discrimination. A friend said to Judge Hoke:

"I consider Dr. Lewis the first citizen of Raleigh."

"Why do you say, 'of Raleigh'?" asked the Judge. "He is the first citizen of the state."

It is good to see that the state was capable of making this judgment for itself. The term "statesman," which was officially and privately applied to this modest physician when he went out of life, shows that North Carolina has learned a new and truer definition of that word which we have so long confused with "politician."

12

Chapter XIX

NORTH CAROLINA'S CROP OF MILLIONAIRES

RECENT statistics indicate that we have almost a hundred millionaires in our state. However true this may be, one thing is certain—few, if any, are millionaires by virtue of descent. They are the beneficiaries of business balances. That is another way of saying that they are self-made or factory-made, in this instance the same thing.

But though the ill fortune of a war which is fast vanishing from our memory prevented any handing-down of riches by family, our new fortunes seem to be building up by families. Examples of course will not prove this theory but they make it plausible enough to write it out. The Dukes—who, on account of the magnitude of their munificence, march at the head of the column—worked together as a family and benefited their neighbors. The Holts, of whose farsighted ancestor I have a dim recollection, fathers, sons, nephews and grandsons, own a score of textile mills. They have worked together in harmony and have carried things before them like an ancient phalanx. So have the Steeles of the Pee Dee. The Reynoldses and the Haneses, working together in family groups, took the products at their doors, made them into what people wanted, and put them on the shelf of every merchant south of the Mason and Dixon line and a vast number north of it. The Sprunts, largest individual cotton exporters in the world, while they have carried our home product to the ends of the earth, have yet maintained their family solidarity and have moved forward together like a small army.

The Wilmington and Weldon Railroad, part of the great Atlantic Coast Line, runs in an almost gradeless tangent across the widest part of North Carolina. Along this railway are strung industries that have made millionaires out of men who have given much more than millions to the eastern section of the state.

The Pattersons, on the Roanoke, resurrected an abandoned canal and poured it into a high class water power, operating cotton mills. The Battles, at the falls of Tar River, reconstructed and amplified mills burnt by the idiocy of war. The Bordens built factories at the crossing of the Neuse and laid out kitchen gardens along the stretch of fifty miles. At the chief seaport of the same river, the Murchisons and McQueens built banks and revived old colonial estates, and the Sprunts not only made history but chronicled it as well.

James Sprunt was a Scotch boy. (The family gave more than a platoon of sons to Britain in the World War. Few of them lived to see the armistice.) He came with his family to the Cape Fear country and began a career which would do credit to any community. Before he was of age he was an officer in the dangerous navigation of blockade running. The handicap of losing a foot did not stay his walk in the paths of diligence. After building up a business which was represented on every continent, he used vacation periods in writing the chronicles of the affable people of the Cape Fear. In years to come he will be blessed for his unselfish disposition in helping others to see what manner of folk were their ancestors. He made his house the home of every guest honored by the city. Three presidents of the United States in turn sat at his table and walked upon the terraces and in the rose gardens overlooking the broad river.

President Wilson, whose father had been the pastor of the First Presbyterian Church, and a part of whose own early life had been spent in the community, was never happier than when talking with Mr. Sprunt in his library. It was in that library, when he was still President of Princeton, that he outlined his intention of some day writing a book which should contain a plan for world peace. He knew that other men had tried this and had failed. But he believed that he had a genuine contribution to make to the discussion and with the enthusiasm of conviction he prophesied to Mr. Sprunt that *his* book would not fail. As it fell out, the crowding events of his later years left no time for writing such a book, but the greater opportunity came to him of writing his plan for peace into the League of Nations; and who shall yet say that his plan has failed?

In Piedmont, leaders were as plentiful as generals in a South American revolution, the difference being that our leaders went somewhere when they led, and had followers.

The Fries family, the Hanes family, and the Gray family were among the founders of the Piedmont's diverse industries. They provided factories to make, transportation to carry, and banks to finance whatever the community could produce.

No one dissenting, the Reynolds family may be called the most enterprising of all the enterprising folk of this region. They led the way, even competing with the great House of Duke. The daring spirit of R. J. Reynolds dominated the industrial spirit of the community and carried the products of its multiplying factories into the markets of the world. There is probably no country on earth where his business does not thrive. Yet he lived and died amongst his neighbors and was himself always essentially a neighbor.

The Reynolds family had come from the flanks of the Virginia mountains to make their home in the Moravian country. It became their home at once; they never had another. They lived contentedly in it and for it. The Reynolds brothers have thought and felt with us and have shared our ever dear prejudices. They have never felt that they must think *for* us, having the old fashioned idea that we could think for ourselves. Neighbors, not nabobs. This, I believe, is the chief reason that the enormous wealth of the family has never barricaded it from the affection of its fellows.

How many multi-millionaires, I wonder, watched the election returns of 1916 with hope in their hearts for Wilson? Very, very few, I fancy, could thus separate themselves from the prejudices of big business. But one who did so separate himself and who identified himself, not with his possessions, but with his people, was Dick Reynolds. He was one of a disconsolate group of us who walked away from the town hall in Winston on that historic night when the early returns from the big eastern centers pointed so plainly to Wilson's defeat. I remember that as we walked along I ventured to say that we had not yet had sufficient returns from the West to make the thing certain, and Dick Reynolds put his hand on my arm and said, "Mr. Peter, you are talking like you hope, not like you think." This was his friendly way of shielding me from further disappointment. It was typical of him. He was always the companion of his friends, enjoying their excitements and sharing their disappointments in the pleasant spirit of a southern town. No wonder, then, that schools and hospitals and churches, things useful and things ornamental to his community, have his memory built into them.

To avoid losing the continuity of the personal touch, I recall the first time that I ever saw James B. Duke. He was a red-headed, freckle-faced citizen of a small town; and at the request of his father he showed me over his new and then pretentious factory. Almost immediately thereafter he began striding along the career which made him a world force in trade; and he is practically lost to personal view.

The gigantic proportions of his success make that success impersonal. One cannot see the freckles on the nose of a giant; all of one's perceptive power is needed to grasp the outline of the great figure.

For the span of a generation he was seldom in the state but the sun never went down upon a day when he was not of the state. When he brought home the spoils of a world trade-conquest, he dumped them almost without reservation into the lap of his mother state. Was not his apparent separation from his people of their making, not his?

If we want to see Mr. Duke through North Carolina eyes, and eyes which are clear sighted enough really to see him, we can look at him in the word picture which Williamson W. Fuller has drawn. Mr. Fuller was indeed the Mæcenas of this Carolina Augustus who turned the very weeds of his native state into gold. From young manhood they were inseparable friends and in the division of their labors it fell to the lot of Mr. Fuller to build the legal structure of the American Tobacco Company after the blue prints of Duke's desires. It later fell to his lot to carry through the more difficult task of taking down the structure and returning each brick to its original place without loss; just as Joseph's brethren found each man the money in the mouth of his sack. Of the many things said in admiration of Mr. Duke, when he lived and when he had ceased to live, none have equaled the truthfulness in which Fuller wrote of him although he wrote before Mr. Duke had concluded his last act of superb generosity.

James Duke had his business before him hung up like a map upon which he could place his fingers on any point to his liking. He was the best bookkeeper of all those employed in that intricate business and it was said of him that if he ever took up an item he never lost it anywhere or anyhow but always knew where it belonged and its relation to the sum total. It is a pleasant thing to be able to say truthfully that of the *literal* legions of men who worked for him no one has ever worked against him. He was little concerned about criticism because he said that if it were deserved, then it would teach him and if it were undeserved, why bother about it?

From his boyhood up, Julian S. Carr's name was abbreviated into Jule Carr. He was, I think, the first North Carolinian who could be called a millionaire by the book. And he made his fortune literally by the sign of the bull. It was not simply for his factories that the Dukes paid him a million dollars. One might almost say that the factories were thrown in for good measure. It was that trade mark of "the Durham Bull" which his industrious genius had painted along the highways of all nations which the Dukes knew they must possess, if they would control the tobacco market.

Jule Carr was one to himself; there was nobody like him. His abundant good nature could not conceal his superficial vanity. Indeed there was no effort to conceal it. It was as patent as the flower he always wore on the lapel of his coat. But it was the unusual sort of vanity that becomes a virtue. A strong dramatic sense gave him his delight in watching himself do good things. And so doing good became an inveterate habit, a constant occupation. He broadcasted kindnesses. It is just possible that he never drilled in deep furrows but he was a most lovable man and it is a delight to one who never had a scrap of paper with Jule's name on it and never stretched his legs under Jule's real mahogany to bear witness to his lovable qualities.

While he was the most popular man in the state—and I think this not an exaggerated judgment—he was never chosen for any public office. As Bourke Cochran said of Grover Cleveland, he was "the most popular man the country over, every day, except election day." But it is characteristic of Jule Carr that he had no hard feelings against fortune for this trick.

Chapter XX

NORTH CAROLINA AND THE SOUTH IN THE AFFAIRS OF THE NATION

THREE decades ago, I came to Washington and took a position in the pay office of the United States Senate. North Carolina was at that time represented by Senators Ransom and Vance, and General Cox was the secretary of the Senate. Vance and Cox have already crossed these pages.

Matt W. Ransom in time of war had been a soldier of brilliant courage. In peace he was a statesman with a talent for subduing danger to the structure of the Government and for promoting commerce and domestic peace. Visitors to Washington today, looking at the broad sweep of the Potomac in those retaining walls which make possible beautiful Potomac Park, can acknowledge their debt to Senator Ransom for securing the legislation which brought about this beauty. He was president of the Senate, as was his distinguished ancestor Nathaniel Macon; and during his long service he was a stately figure in the senatorial body. He had a presence of manly beauty, a rare eloquence, and an elegance of manner which placed him among the leaders of a great legislative body in great times.

During my thirty odd years in Washington, I have watched the ever increasing stride of North Carolina with an affection and pride that separation could only deepen. But necessarily I have watched from a distance, through a telescope as it were. It would be absurd for me

to attempt to record events which have already been recorded by men who were on the spot with microscopes.
I shall therefore do no more than suggest the telescopic
angle of vision.

At long range, it has at least been possible to measure
the orbit of North Carolina's brightest political planet.

Furnifold M. Simmons, measured by actual achievements, is the greatest representative North Carolina has
ever sent to the councils of the nation. His word has
literally become law for a hundred million people. He is
accepted, without cavil, by his fellow senators as a statesman in the best meaning of that misused word. And he
has been genuinely representative of his people who early
escaped from the after-war menace of demagoguery and
learned the wisdom of doing big things quietly.

The Finance Committee of the United States Senate
is one of the engines which enable our Government to
run; and Senator Simmons, as Chairman of the Committee, was the engineer in control when the machinery of
government was put to the supreme test of a World War.
The successful legislative financing of that war will cause
the name of Furnifold Simmons to be written into the
headlines of history. His is the system of taxation which,
in the last decade, has brought into the national treasury
almost thirty billions of dollars.*

When the Democrats lost control of Congress in 1918,
Senator Simmons ceased to be chairman of the Finance
Committee, but it is a matter of record that his superior
understanding of fiscal and economic questions has

---

*The excess profits tax which was sponsored by Senator Simmons, according
to the calculations of experts at the Treasury Department, brought into the
United States Treasury more money in one year than any other tax has ever
raised in the history of the world.

enabled him in more than one critical time to direct the
Senate's taxation policy from the minority side.

Perhaps his most renowned victory was the defeat of
the so-called Mellon plan of taxation in 1921-22. The
national propaganda for the Mellon plan assumed proportions which made any opposition seem futile. Yet
Senator Simmons continued to fight day after day for a
substitute bill which would lift the grievous burden of
taxation from the poor taxpayer before it lifted the burden from the broad shoulders of the rich. In his simple,
quiet way he made such a strong case that he won to his
side not only all the Democrats but a sufficient number
of liberal Republicans to adopt his bill, rather than the
Administration plan. It was a remarkable and a decisive
victory and the resultant prosperity in the country justified
his course. But for neither the victory nor the prosperity
has he been given the meed of credit that is his, because
the great publicity machine which he defeated still func-
tioned strongly enough to muffle the reports of the
contest.

The Finance Committee has not been the only scene
of Mr. Simmons's senatorial labors. He has served on
the Committee on Commerce for eleven Congresses,
where his service has been productive of increased and
increasing commerce, especially along the South Atlantic
Seaboard. His interests and his talents lead him into
constructive legislation, rather than oratorical contests;
he is far more concerned with insuring an unobstructed
flow for our inland waterways than in adding to the flood
of oratory which daily swishes through the halls of Congress. And for that reason his reputation is safe with the
future; it will live as long as men value a practical, work-
able Democracy.

Senator Lee Slater Overman, the junior senator from
North Carolina, is now in his fifth term. There has been
published in the Biographical History of distinguished
North Carolinians a full sketch of his public services,
which I wrote, and therefore a further discussion of his
career in these pages would be a repetition on my part.
The acts of Congress which bear his name, important war
measures, are permanent records of his more recent distinguished services.

It may not be too much to claim that in Washington
one learns to measure not only the contribution which
North Carolina makes to the nation, but the contribution
of the South as a whole.

It seemed almost a miracle to see that aged taunt of
the Republicans—"The Democrats will put the South in
the saddle"—turned into a proud fact at the most crucial
moment of modern history. The South *was* in the saddle
when our country entered the World War. And the success of its horsemanship is written into history too deeply
to be disturbed or distorted.

Woodrow Wilson cannot, with truth, be claimed as
more than fractionally a southerner. And that southern
fraction was not strong enough to affect his thought
which was not merely national but international. Yet
one thing was indelibly written upon Woodrow Wilson's
character by his early southern environment. That thing
was an understanding of the unreality of defeat. It was
my privilege to be in the room with him at a moment
when he startlingly dramatized his refusal to accept the
implications of defeat.

The occasion was that tragic March 4, 1921, and the
time very close to twelve o'clock noon. Mr. Wilson was

in the President's room at the Capitol where he had come
in accordance with custom for the last minute signing of
such bills as should meet his approval; and there were
present the usual number of persons who had come to
pay their respects to him. Then there entered Senator
Lodge and Senator Underwood, leaders of the major
parties in the Senate, to announce to the President that
the Senate of the Sixty-sixth Congress had concluded its
labors. Mr. Lodge was the spokesman for the committee
and while he merely repeated the perfunctory words of
his announcement, to the effect that if the President had
no further communication to make, the Senate stood
ready to adjourn, yet there was an implication in his
intonation and in his manner which left no one in any
doubt that he found very pleasant that accident of fate
which had made him the one to take from this fallen
leader the sword of authority.

The President, standing erect and looking at Mr. Lodge
as though he were not, replied—

"I have no further communication to make,"
and with a gesture of the head, indescribable, but understood the world over, Mr. Wilson dismissed him. Lodge
held in his hands all the tangible proofs of victory, but
it was not Lodge who left that room the victor.

Immediately after this, leaning heavily on his cane,
Mr. Wilson walked down the long corridor, lined with
curious onlookers, to the elevator. When he got out of
the elevator, he put his hand on the shoulder of the elevator boy for a little help in making the step. As he left,
he turned to this boy and said, "Thank you, my son, for
your assistance."

With this gentle "vale," Woodrow Wilson passed from
public life and in that infinitesimal time which elapses

between the death of an outgoing administration and the birth of the incoming one, he became the foremost private citizen of the world.

I like to believe that it was those years of his youth which he spent in the South, some of them on the banks of our own Cape Fear River, which taught Woodrow Wilson the knowledge which he clasped to his breast in his last years,—knowledge that while to the victor belong the material spoils, to the vanquished may belong the treasures of the spirit. He grew noticeably in spiritual stature after he had been physically laid low. Defeat gave him her most shining gifts and crowned him.

All the gifts which defeat makes to her children are not good gifts, however. Out of the very sympathy and unity which a vanquished people develop there may grow a tyranny of prejudice. That has happened to us in the South and in North Carolina as a part of the South. We faced after the Civil War a menace which can scarcely be exaggerated,—a cherished grudge which was bent on forcing us into political bondage and social degradation. In all the world we saw but one friendly hand stretched out to help us. That was the hand of the Democratic party. Against the bitter prejudice of their neighbors, the Democrats of the North fought the battle for fair play toward a prostrate people; and it shames us to forget that of these Democrats, Tammany Wigwam fought without profit or fear for our salvation. We in the South clutched at this helpful hand extended to us and were led by it to higher fighting ground. There we have, of necessity, clung together. Individualists have been dangerous to the general safety; mutiny has been promptly punished. Our political solidarity has been an essential and a right thing.

But out of it there has grown an insistence upon a parallel intellectual solidarity which ought not to be. We punish intellectual pioneers as we punish political renegades. And strangely enough this mass domination of thought has led us in a vicious circle to a queer sort of political ingratitude. Our people have of late insisted on a peculiar brand of ecclesiastical politics and they have been taught by ignorant leaders to distrust all Democrats in the North who would like to worship God according to a different formula from theirs, or who happen to hold more liberal views on the question of what we shall eat or what we shall drink. The strange and violent tales which are told to our people about the wickedness of Catholics and the baseness of anti-prohibitionists are of a piece with the tales which fifty years ago were told about our own "cruelties" to the people whose worst crime was the fact that they were blacks. And the new tales are no truer than those old tales. It is a sad ingratitude that we should believe lies about the very people who believed the truth about us.

There has grown up among younger southerners a strong little army of independent and philosophic thinkers. In North Carolina we have a whole regiment of them, led by that delightful Amazon, Nell Battle Lewis. They are doing a brave and a fine thing in breaking their lances against prejudice. They will get much sympathy from us oldsters. Viewing them from a distance both in space and time, however, I would insert one little word of caution. I would urge them, in repairing the ladder by which we have climbed to our present security, not to kick the ladder completely over. Perhaps a little story of other times will best embody this cautious reminder.

The story begins and ends with Dr. George W. Black-nall, openhanded host of the Yarborough House, who, for his fair speech, was nicknamed "Sugar lips," by an editor who had much facility in this art. In a decline of his fortunes, Dr. Blacknall became a collector of internal revenue at Raleigh. The moonshiners of the period had grown so bold that almost within sight of the dome of the Capitol they had fired too accurately at some revenue officers and had bagged a brace of them. The most excellent majesty of the Government had to be asserted and Dr. Blacknall was sent to use his gifts in composing the trouble.

On his way through a dark swamp at the bend of the road, he was confronted by a parcel of country-looking folk, singularly well ·supplied with fowling pieces. The doctor, who was driving along in his buggy, softly whistling to himself, as was his custom, was not in the least dismayed. When the strangers suggested to him that his safest plan was to turn his horse's head and drive back whence he had come, he said:

"Gentlemen, you make a great mistake. I have not come amongst you as an enemy but I am sent as a messenger. I am just from Washington where I saw Grover Cleveland about our troubles and he told me to come back and tell you that while he sympathized with you, he had to carry out the law of the land, and that if you would persist in making moonshine, then wouldn't you please move back just a leetle further from the road."

Those of us who have come along the highway when it was rockiest would warn our young rebels, in old Dr. Blacknall's words, to move just a "leetle further from the road" when they begin mixing dangerous ingredients.

But such advice is, after all, beside the point. For they are entering on a new day and it is their day. A glorious one, I believe it will prove. But no happier, I know, than the day we snatched from the very jaws of destitution and oppression; the day we snatched and ran away with, to fill it with comradeship and reckless fun and friendship.

"Tenderly, day that I have loved, I close your eyes."

INDEX